SO-BEI-185

COMPREHENSIVE RESEARCH
AND STUDY GUIDE

# A.E. Housman

EDITED AND WITH AN INTRODUCTION
BY HAROLD BLOOM

# CURRENTLY AVAILABLE

COMPREHENSIVE RESEARCH
AND STUDY GUIDE

# A.E. Housman

CHELSEA HOUSE
PUBLISHERS
A Haights Cross Communications Company

Philadelphia

# BLOOM'S *MAJOR* POETS

EDITED AND WITH AN INTRODUCTION
BY HAROLD BLOOM

© 2003 by Chelsea House Publishers, a subsidiary of
Haights Cross Communications.

A Haights Cross Communications ✦ Company

Introduction © 2003 by Harold Bloom.

Printed and bound in the United States of America.

First Printing
1 3 5 7 9 8 6 4 2

Library of Congress Cataloging-in-Publication Data

A.E. Housman / edited and with an introduction by Harold Bloom.
     p. cm. — (Bloom's major poets)
Includes bibliographical references and index.
  ISBN 0-7910-7392-0
  1. Housman, A. E. (Alfred Edward), 1859-1936—Criticism and
interpretation.  I. Bloom, Harold. II. Series.
  PR4809.H15Z525 2003
  821'.912—dc21

                                                    2003001604


Chelsea House Publishers
1974 Sproul Road, Suite 400
Broomall, PA 19008-0914

www.chelseahouse.com

Contributing Editor: Lisa Hirschfield

Cover design by Terry Mallon

Layout by EJB Publishing Services

# CONTENTS

# AN INDEX TO POEMS
# IN THIS VOLUME

# USER'S GUIDE

This volume is designed to present biographical, critical, and bibliographical information on the author and the author's best-known or most important poems. Following Harold Bloom's editor's note and introduction is a concise biography of the author that discusses major life events and important literary accomplishments. A critical analysis of each poem follows, tracing significant themes, patterns, and motifs in the work. As with any study guide, it is recommended that the reader read the poem beforehand, and have a copy of the poem being discussed available for quick reference.

A selection of critical extracts, derived from previously published material, follows each thematic analysis. In most cases, these extracts represent the best analysis available from a number of leading critics. Because these extracts are derived from previously published material, they will include the original notations and references when available. Each extract is cited, and readers are encouraged to check the original publication as they continue their research. A bibliography of the author's writings, a list of additional books and articles on the author and their work, and an index of themes and ideas conclude the volume.

# ABOUT THE EDITOR

**Harold Bloom** is Sterling Professor of the Humanities at Yale University and Henry W. and Albert A. Berg Professor of English at the New York University Graduate School. He is the author of over 20 books, and the editor of more than 30 anthologies of literary criticism.

Professor Bloom's works include *Shelley's Mythmaking* (1959), *The Visionary Company* (1961), *Blake's Apocalypse* (1963), *Yeats* (1970), *A Map of Misreading* (1975), *Kabbalah and Criticism* (1975), *Agon: Toward a Theory of Revisionism* (1982), *The American Religion* (1992), *The Western Canon* (1994), and *Omens of Millennium: The Gnosis of Angels, Dreams, and Resurrection* (1996). *The Anxiety of Influence* (1973) sets forth Professor Bloom's provocative theory of the literary relationships between the great writers and their predecessors. His most recent books include *Shakespeare: The Invention of the Human*, a 1998 National Book Award finalist, *How to Read and Why* (2000), and *Genius: A Mosaic of One Hundred Exemplary Creative Minds* (2002).

Professor Bloom earned his Ph.D. from Yale University in 1955 and has served on the Yale faculty since then. He is a 1985 MacArthur Foundation Award recipient and served as the Charles Eliot Norton Professor of Poetry at Harvard University in 1987–88. In 1999 he was awarded the prestigious American Academy of Arts and Letters Gold Medal for Criticism. Professor Bloom is the editor of several other Chelsea House series in literary criticism, including BLOOM'S MAJOR SHORT STORY WRITERS, BLOOM'S MAJOR NOVELISTS, BLOOM'S MAJOR DRAMATISTS, BLOOM'S MODERN CRITICAL INTERPRETATIONS, BLOOM'S MODERN CRITICAL VIEWS, and BLOOM'S BIOCRITIQUES.

# EDITOR'S NOTE

My Introduction is a brief critical defense of Housman's poetry.

Of the numerous critical views excerpted here, those by the late Cleanth Brooks and by Christopher Ricks have a particular authority.

I would also commend the scholarship brought to Housman studies by B.J. Leggett, Tom Burns Haber, and Keith Jebb. But all of the excerpts in this little volume make contributions to a better understanding of A.E. Housman's lasting achievement.

# Harold Bloom

Edmund Wilson was a remarkable critic, but not necessarily of modern poetry. In the decline of his former lover, the Byronic Edna St. Vincent Millay, Wilson found the debacle of modern verse. Against A.E. Housman, Wilson got off the grim shot: "Housman has managed to grow old without in a sense knowing maturity." Cyril Connolly was a touch nastier: "He will live as long as the B.B.C." Tom Stoppard, in his *The Birth of Love*, has juxtaposed Housman with Oscar Wilde, much to Wilde's favor.

As a reader of Housman's poetry since childhood, I tend to be surprised by critical dislike of his work. Housman palpably is not a poet of the eminence of Thomas Hardy and D.H. Lawrence, of Edward Thomas and Wilfred Owen, of T.S. Eliot and Geoffrey Hill, and W.B. Yeats is a mountain range of excellence away. But I greatly prefer Housman to many poets who support critical industries (Pound, Auden, *et al*), and I am puzzled how any lover of poetry could fail to respond to this:

> Into my heart an air that kills
>   From yon far country blows:
> What are those blue remembered hills,
>   What spires, what farms are those?
>
> That is the land of lost content,
>   I see it shining plain,
> The happy highways where I went
>   And cannot come again.

The first line: "Into my heart an air that kills" is almost a poem in itself, and is a superb irony. It seems strange that Housman should be so undervalued as an ironist. As a classicist, he tends to favor the irony that says one thing while meaning another, but he is also a Romantic ironist, with a keen sense that meaning breaks under the strain of the irony of irony. "The Land of Lost Content" is precisely what cannot be seen, but Housman risks the Blakean line: "I see it shining plain."

Housman, though he can have a superficial resemblance to the earlier Blake, is anything but a visionary poet. Tom Stoppard, in his brilliant *The Invention of Love*, tells us that Housman's life was a failure, in contrast to Oscar Wilde's. Housman probably would have agreed with Stoppard, but recovering from an open heart operation makes me very wary of terming anyone's life a failure.

Do failures write uncanny poems? I have been upset with one of Housman's poems for longer than I can remember:

> Her strong enchantments failing,
>   Her towers of fear in wreck,
> Her limbecks dried of poisons
>   And the knife at her neck,
>
> The Queen of air and darkness
>   Begins to shrill and cry,
> 'O young man, O my slayer,
>   To-morrow you shall die.'
>
> O Queen of air and darkness,
>   I think 'tis truth you say,
> And I shall die to-morrow;
>   But you will die to-day.

The Queen of air and darkness is no ordinary witch, and her young slayer is grimmer than any irony. What is the poem for? What did Housman do for himself, whether as person or as poet, by composing this poem? He was not susceptible to female enchantments, however strong, and this morbid little masterpiece of a lyric appears to have no sexual element, as it would if we found it in Kipling or in William Morris, or in the sado-masochistic Swinburne: One feels that Housman is exorcising something, something he cannot quite confront.

If I had to choose only one poem by Housman, it would be the superbly savage "Epitaph upon an Army of Mercenaries." But his subtlest and most beautiful poem probably is this:

> Tell me not here, it needs not saying,
>   What tune the enchantress plays
> In aftermaths of soft September
>   Or under blanching mays,
> For she and I were long acquainted
>   And I knew all her ways.

On russet floors, by waters idle,
  The pine lets fall its cone;
The cuckoo shouts all day at nothing
  In leafy dells alone;
And traveller's joy beguiles in autumn
  Hearts that have lost their own.

On acres of the seeded grasses
  The changing burnish heaves;
Or marshalled under moons of harvest
  Stands still all night the sheaves;
Or beeches strip in storms for winter
  And stain the wind with leaves.

Possess, as I possessed a season,
  The countries I resign,
Where over elmy plains the highway
  Would mount the hills and shine,
And full of shade the pillared forest
  Would murmur and be mine.

For nature, heartless, witless nature,
  Will neither care nor know
What stranger's feet may find the meadow
  And trespass there and go,
Nor ask amid the dews of morning
  If they are mine or no.

Had Ben Jonson lived to read this, he might have said: "Had the poet intended an actual mistress, it would have been something." The poem's language is certainly the most heteroerotic in all of Housman, who nevertheless follows Wordsworthian convention by personifying nature as a beloved woman. Yet Housman's enchantress is "heartless, witless," and this is a poem of loss, of intimations of mortality. But there is magnificence in the loss, and an erotic music of the unlived life.

# A.E. Housman

Alfred Edward Housman was born on March 26, 1859 in Fockbury, England. In his early childhood, the family moved to Catshill, Worcestershire, within sight of the Shropshire hills. Housman was the oldest of seven siblings, among whom included Laurence, who became a well-known dramatist, and his sister Clemence, who became a novelist and short-story writer. When Housman was twelve, his mother died, initiating a gradual but definitive loss of religious faith; his disillusioned atheism would become a great influence on his poetry. He attended the Bromsgrove School, well known for its classical curriculum, and between 1877–1881, St. John's College, Oxford, where he read Classics, another significant poetic influence. Although Housman gained honors for his first examination in Classics, he failed in his final examination—Greats, or *Litterae Humaniores*—in 1881, and left Oxford that summer without a final degree.

After returning to Oxford in the fall of that year to earn a "pass" degree, Housman took the Civil Service Exam. He then moved to London to work in the Royal Patent Office. During this time, Housman continued to read and study Classics in the British Museum. This proved fruitful, for he published widely on the subject, and became a formidable classical scholar during the ten years he worked as a civil servant. In 1892, Housman was appointed Professor of Latin at University College, London, where he taught until 1911. Despite his reclusive nature, during the latter part of his career at UCL, Housman socialized regularly with a small and select number of friends, who included his brother Laurence and his publisher Grant Richards. Known to be a connoisseur of fine food and wine, and a brilliant and witty conversationalist, he nevertheless continued to isolate himself from the London literati, and had little interest in his contemporary writers, such as Eliot, Yeats, and Joyce. In 1911, Housman was elected Kennedy Professor of Latin at Cambridge University, and became a Fellow of Trinity College. He gained acceptance to an elite faculty clique at Cambridge, but true to his nature, refrained from developing any close relationships there. Housman continued to teach at Cambridge through the mid-nineteen-thirties. Long-suffering from heart disease, he died in Cambridge on October 30, 1936.

In 1896, the first edition of *A Shropshire Lad* was published, not long after Housman's difficulties at Oxford. He later described this period as one of "continuous excitement"; in this phase of industrious activity, he wrote both *A Shropshire Lad* and many of the verses that would appear later in *Last Poems*. Housman's baffling failure at Oxford was subject to much speculation both before and after his death. His diaries later revealed that during this period he had become extremely despondent over a relationship with a fellow student, Moses Jackson, with whom he shared rooms. In 1882, Housman again shared lodgings in London with Jackson and Jackson's brother, Adalbert. There has been some speculation that he had romantic attachments to both men. However, Housman's realization of his homosexuality, coupled with Moses Jackson's rejection, threw him into a state of reclusiveness and introversion, which would come to predominate both his life and his poetry. Indeed, Housman's contemporaries described him as an "enigmatic personality burdened by a private grief."

During his years in the Civil Service, at UCL, and at Cambridge, Housman published prolifically on classical literature, translated and edited the works of major classical writers, and produced literary criticism as well, including *The Name and the Nature of Poetry*. Yet his poetic oeuvre was relatively small. He was quoted by his publisher Grant Richards to declare "I am not a poet by trade. I am a professor of Latin." Undeniably, Housman's poetic productivity declined significantly after the publication of *A Shropshire Lad*. However, in 1922, twenty-six years after *A Shropshire Lad*—and the same year of T.S. Eliot's *The Waste Land*—he published *Last Poems*. Many of the poems in this volume were written in the 1890's. Other poems reflect the Edwardian period, and still others, the Boer War—in which his younger brother Herbert was killed—and World War I. By its very title, it is clear that Housman intended this volume of poems to serve as an epitaph to his poetic career.

However, in 1936, Housman's brother Laurence posthumously edited and published *More Poems*, followed in 1937 with a memoir that included *Additional Poems*. Nearly all of the pieces in these volumes were written during Housman's most prolific period, but not included in the earlier publications. As his brother's literary executor, Laurence chose to publish some of Housman's most emotionally frank poems. He justified this by claiming that he had the power and responsibility to do for his brother in death what

Housman could not, or would not, do for himself in life. Several of the poems in *More Poems* refer openly to Housman's homosexuality and describe a thwarted romantic relationship. Given his emotional and social reticence, it is no wonder that Housman suppressed these poems during his lifetime.

Socially reclusive yet well-traveled; cold in manner yet passionate in temperament; a prominent, influential scholar and critic who routinely declined honors and awards; a sharp, sparkling conversationalist who wrote spare, taciturn verse, Housman seemed an aggregate of paradoxes in his lifetime, and today he remains an enigmatic figure in English literary history. Such irreconcilable differences are evident in Housman's small but powerful body of work as well. *A Shropshire Lad*'s simplicity of subject, introspective tone, and restrained feeling belies its sophisticated prosody, plurality of voice, and emotional complexity. Its more superficial qualities made the work unlike most contemporaneous late-Victorian verse, and *A Shropshire Lad* was not an immediate best-seller. Nevertheless, over time its popularity, and that of its author, grew. By the time of *Last Poems*'s publication in 1922, Alfred Edward Housman had become one of the most widely-read poets of his generation.

# THE DIVIDED PERSONA OF HOUSMAN

## CRITICAL ANALYSIS OF

# *A Shropshire Lad* 2, 58, and 62

The theme of a divided person, or split subjectivity, is pervasive throughout Housman's poetry. A great many of his poems clearly convey such a division in feeling, tone, voice, or figuration of selfhood.

Time is of the essence in much of Housman's poetry. In these particular poems, figurations of time manifest themselves in terms of the speaker's age and point of view, in the differences between "then" and "now," in his recognition of mortality and the inevitability of death, as well as in his apprehension of seemingly endless cycles of nature. A sense of sadness, regret, and alienation is woven throughout these poems. The speaker's awareness of time and change conflict with an implicit desire to control circumstances. Such an untenable position steers the speaker toward a sense of alienation and regret, and thus into the fragmentation in feeling or persona that so often distinguishes Housman's poetry.

Take, for example, *A Shropshire Lad* 2, "Loveliest of trees, the cherry now. While it concludes with an optimistic determination to experience the world as much as possible in "fifty springs," this determination has arisen from a sense of loss. At the young age of twenty, the poet already feels a keen awareness of his mortality and even a sadness for what cannot be retrieved. "Twenty will not come again": When compared to the seemingly timeless resurrection of the natural world (as suggested by "Eastertide" as well as springtime), we humans cannot endure the centuries. Unlike what can be resurrected, we are mortal, and each of our lives on earth is finite. This glancing reference to Christianity underscores Housman's secularity, his avowed disbelief in any human incarnation of the infinite. Many critics have found this point of view consistent with what they consider Housman's pessimism; it may also be read as evidence of a thoroughly modern, post-Darwinist realism.

Although the poem suggests the poet's desire to experience life for as long as is possible, it is laced with his sense of mortality and the finite, which is where the poem finds its tension. The somewhat lighter, almost optimistic tone of the final stanza contrasts with the jaded voice of the middle stanza; the images of flowering trees and springtime in the first conflict with the speaker's morbid fascination with his eventual death in the last. Moreover, the flowering cherry is an image of the cyclical, yet impermanent, present, contrasted with the finitude of the poet's life. While the snowlike blossoms on the bough will soon enough be replaced with real snow, they will return again. However, the poet will now have one less spring, and he cannot hope to return forever with each Eastertide.

The poet's relationship to life and death are reiterated in *A Shropshire Lad* 58. "When I came last to Ludlow," the bonds of friendship and, by extension, a stable social world were intact. Upon the speaker's return, all has changed. One friend is dead, the other has committed a crime and "lies long in jail." Clearly, that world of social relationships has not remained stable, and it seems almost as if the poet's absence has some connection to this disintegration. The final lines, "and I come home to Ludlow / Amidst the moonlight pale," highlight the speaker's current alienation from his former world and the sense of separation and difference his absence has engendered. The image of a single man, his face pale in the moonlight, is haunting. We can almost see a sense of defeat in his posture, and his shocked expression.

In this poem, division is marked by a rift in the continuity of social and emotional bonds, as well as by the juxtaposition of "then" and "now." However, the tension created between the two stanzas arises from not from the sense of difference, but from the one thing that has remained stable: the speaker's perspective. He comes, he goes, but until now his relationship to Ludlow and to its people have not changed, and he has measured himself by that constancy. Now he returns to find that all has changed but him. It is this transformation and the alienation that results which threaten to destabilize the poet's point of view—especially his sense of self.

A divided point of view and the poet's split subjectivity, or selfhood, seem the very subject of *A Shropshire Lad* 62, "Terence, this is stupid stuff." Terence Hearsay, the poet and speaker in *Shropshire*, is having a conversation—or rather, an argument—with an unidentified friend. While we might easily conclude that this is a dialogue within Housman's own mind about the relevance of poetry, it is also an exchange of ideas between Terence the poet and a Shropshire lad—an erudite, ambitious realist, and a local "lad" like the Dick or Tom of *Shropshire* 58. An uncharacteristically long poem for Housman, *Shropshire* 62 is also unusual because it is a dialogue in rhyming couplets. Not only is Housman invoking the classical Greek form of pastoral, in his use of the four-stressed line (tetrameter) he is playing with the "rustic" English ballad tradition. Both forms are fitting modes of versification in Housman's imagined Shropshire.

*Shropshire* 62 is also about the uses of both poetry and of pessimism—how both can work as a kind of tonic against unrealizable hopes and ideals, a vaccination against life's disappointments. The final verse paragraph retells the story of Mithradates (spelled incorrectly by Housman), an ancient Near Eastern ruler who failed in an attempt to poison himself after his troops revolted. In the popular myth that Housman cites, the king took poison in small quantities until he had built up such a resistance that he became impervious to its effects.

*Shropshire* 62 begins with the friend's invitation to Terence: to put off the world-weariness of his verse and "pipe a tune to dance to, lad." Terence replies that poetry is not written pleasure, which can be had more easily through drink. "Ale, man, ale's the stuff to drink / For fellows whom it hurts to think." And yet even this sort of pleasure is merely the means for delusion; it is only a temporary stay against life's troubles, while poetry can offer gifts more enduring. "Look into the pewter pot / To see the world as the world's not." In the second verse paragraph, Terence justifies his point of view and the motivation behind his verse:

> Luck's a chance, but trouble's sure,
> I'd face it as a wise man would,
> And train for ill and not for good.
> 'Tis true, the stuff I bring for sale
> Is not so brisk a brew as ale:
> Out of a stem that scored the hand
> I wrung it in a weary land. ....
>
> It should do good to heart and head
> When your soul is in my soul's stead;
> And I will friend you, if I may,
> In the dark and cloudy day.

Conflating images of brewing, writing, and the landscape, "Out of a stem that scored the hand / I wrung it in a weary land" conveys the poet's emotional strife. Scoring suggests writing, yet he has scored (or scarred) his own writing hand with branches of hops, grown in this "weary land." It is as if this astringent poetry was meant to fortify Housman's Shropshire, but this has also come at a personal cost. The sense of sacrifice and the hard work of the rural laborer is reiterated in "wrung" and "weary."

This sour brew is not only offered to the friend as a mental tonic; it becomes a token of identification, a means of sympathy, and a mode of emotional exchange in times to come. This conflates the two voices/personae in the future tense, but reinforces their differences in the present. Terence, the once-alienated cynic, can be generous and sympathetic once he is understood: "When your soul is in my soul's stead," he says, "I will friend you." The use of "friend" as a verb in this line is interesting, for it turns feeling and thought into potential action. Desire for emotional and physical connection, and the fraught relationship of thought to action in this regard, are common themes in Housman's work, which often blur the lines between the biographical A.E. Housman and the voice of his poems, Terence Hearsay.

# *A Shropshire Lad* 2, 58, and 62

## ELLEN FRIEDMAN ON HOUSMAN'S "DIVIDED SELF"

[Ellen Friedman is co-editor of The *Review of Contemporary Fiction*, and has published many books and articles on women's writing. She is Professor of English and Director of the Women's and Gender Studies Program at The College of New Jersey. Ms. Friedman identifies Housman's "divided self" in *A Shropshire Lad* 58 and *More Poems* 6. She argues that Housman "uses the rhetoric of irony"—that is, the play of opposites—to delineate these personae, creating different points of view, and complicating the seemingly pastoral world in which they operate.]

In poem after poem A. E. Housman uses the rhetoric of irony to express the grim vision that life's joys are won in vain since they must all dissolve in death. The images of pastoral peace, of beautiful Shropshire lads and lasses, of brave soldiers full of patriotic purpose which Housman conjures up at the beginning of a poem are dispelled by the end of the poem. This characteristic is evident in "When I Came Last to Ludlow" (*ASL* 58):[1]

> When I came last to Ludlow
>     Amidst the moonlight pale,
> Two friends kept step beside me,
>     Two honest lads and hale.
>
> Now Dick lies long in the churchyard,
>     And Ned lies long in jail,
> And I come home to Ludlow
>     Amidst the moonlight pale.

The short, two stanza structure is a most effective vehicle for the use of ironic reversal. In the first stanza we encounter warm comradeship, but in the second stanza we find only death and loss. This pattern of life and loss is repeated throughout the Housman canon (see *LP* 11, 15, 20, 21, 22, 23, 27, 28 for some striking examples).

This technique of ironic reversal or, perhaps more accurately, shift in perception is not limited to the two-stanza poems. It is an obsessive quality in the Housman canon. However, these ironic shifts describing the movement from life to loss in Housman's poetry disguise another, almost opposing movement. In many of the poems there is an underlying, muted, mostly hidden celebration of the loss by the speaker who has somehow survived it. This "celebration" is effected in defense, by a painful process of self-isolation and depersonalization, often by an objectification of everything that is not the speaker. It is a separation that may be seen in terms of R. D. Laing's theories of the schizoid (as distinguished from the mental illness, schizophrenia). Laing states:

> The term schizoid refers to an individual the totality of whose experience is split in two main ways: In the first place, there is a rent in his relation with his world, and in the second, there is a disruption of his relation with himself. Such a person is not able to experience himself "together with" others or "at home in" the world, but on the contrary, he experiences himself in despairing aloneness and isolation; moreover, he does not experience himself as a complete person but rather as a mind more or less tenuously inked to a body, as two or more selves, and so on.[2]

In the light of Laing's theories, Housman's poems take on an interesting dimension. Let us take a closer look at the poem "When I Came Last to Ludlow" referred to above. The poem depicts the fate of the narrator's two friends. Although we feel regret for the change in the three friends' circumstance, and we generalize this regret to all experience, this feeling is not a result of a mood the narrator projects. It is a feeling we automatically bring to the poem in response to the facts presented. The feelings of regret, loss, loneliness; the realization of the transience and mutability of existence well up within us, and we naturally feed these feelings into the poem. However, the narrator expresses no such feeling. The lack of this feeling in the poem, when we disengage ourselves from it, is striking, even startling. There is a divorce between the events and their meaning that suggests Laing's description of the schizoid's fear of engulfments:

In this the individual dreads relatedness as such, with anyone or anything or, indeed, even with himself.... The manoeuvre [sic] used to preserve identity under pressure from the dread of engulfment is isolation.[3]

When seen in this psychological light, "When I Came Last to Ludlow," reveals another facet: The repeated first and last lines, "When I came last to Ludlow / Amidst the moonlight pale," act as a frame and carry the banner to stability and autonomy while the pictures which change within that frame ("Two friends kept step beside me, / Two honest lads and hale, / Now Dick lies long in the churchyard / And Ned lies long in jail") emphasize, by contrasting with the framing lines, the independence the speaker has achieved from his engulfment by the stream of life and time. This establishment of independence is a response to loss, a defensive self-isolation. The poem in this view is an establishment of the integrity of the self in the face of change and impermanence.

Although Housman uses the idiom of soldiers and country lads and lasses, his seeming lack of emotion gives us a clue to one source of meaning in Housman's poetry. Housman's Shropshire character continually laments the loss of friends and lovers; but beneath the depressive movement, there is an ascending one, a movement created to transcend the harsh realities the poems' surfaces describe, where the sound of the lament serves to reassure the speaker of the reality, the substantiality of at least his own voice.

## NOTES

1. The following abbreviations are used in referring to the books in the Housman canon; *ASL* (*A Shropshire Lad*), *LP* (*Last Poems*), *MP* (*More Poems*), *AP* (*Additional Poems*); all quotations from the poems are made from *The Collected Poems of A. E. Housman* (NY: Holt, Rinehart & Winston, 1971).
2. R. D. Laing, *The Divided Self* (NY: Random House, 1969), p. 15.
3. Ibid, p. 46.

—Ellen Friedman, "The Divided Self in the Poems of A.E. Housman." *English Literature in Transition, 1880–1920* Vol. 20:1, 1977: pp. 27–29.

## Miriam B. Mandel on Ambiguity of Action in "Loveliest of Trees"

[Professor Miriam B. Mandel teaches at Tel Aviv University. She has been working on a three-volume encyclopedia of Hemingway's works, and is on the editorial board of *The Hemingway Review*. Her close reading of *A Shropshire Lad* 2, "Loveliest of trees," explores the poem's play of opposites in terms of the *vita contempletiva* and the *vita activa*—the life of passive thought versus that of direct action—a Classical literary trope.]

The recent enthusiasm for a close if sometimes deconstructive way of reading a text has caused critics to discard 'the notion ... that the simplicity and directness of Housman's poetry obviates the necessity for close analysis' (Leggett *Land* 4). Christopher Ricks and B.J. Leggett, among others, have identified previously unsuspected complexities, tensions and contradictions in a number of Housman's poems; 'Loveliest of trees' has also benefited from this close attention. Subjecting it to a very rigorous reading, Leggett was able to distinguish the sophisticated voice of the poet from that of the naive speaker. Leggett concludes that the poet and the persona, though distinguishable, are not conflicting or contradictory: each fulfils a different function, but together they work to create a single effect. Leggett finds, therefore, that 'Loveliest of trees' is 'one of the most straightforward of the poems of *A Shropshire Lad*, ('Insight' 329). ( ... )

It seems to me, however, that the situation in this poem is rather more complex than scholars have realised: in 'Loveliest of trees' the poem seems to be working not to support but to undermine the speaker. Although the created persona seems an earnest and sincere youth, the poem itself undermines both the speaker and his argument.

Housman's speaker does seem to be extremely attractive. He is a sensitive and intelligent observer of nature: Housman emphasises both his awareness and the correctness of his evaluation of the cherry tree by presenting them in the first word of the poem. Although unsophisticated, he seems a balanced character, avoiding the extreme of sentimental enthusiasm as well as the gloomy pessimism so prevalent among Housman's speakers. His realistic awareness that time is short and death inevitable evokes in him a positive response: 'instead of producing a languid pessimism in the face of certain death, the realisation of his transience results in an intensification of the speaker's perception' (Leggett *Land* 16). The attractive character of the speaker seems to reinforce the affirmative tone of the poem. His youthfulness (he is twenty years old) and the season of the poem (spring, Eastertime) add overtones of optimism and energy to the already positive atmosphere. The poem ends with a strong, insistent call for action appropriate to the *carpe diem* genre, to the spring, and to the youth of the speaker: the 'emphasis is on living life fully *now*' (Perrine 27). In this poem, then, there seems to be no 'split between the personals attitude and the attitude of the poem as a whole' (Leggett 'Insight' 336).

But when we examine what the poem actually represents we find that 'Loveliest of trees' is indeed torn by internal contradiction. Both the speaker's actions and his inaction contradict the ideas he expresses: the way he thinks is not consistent with either his conclusions or the way he presents them. This 'tug of contraries' (Ricks 271) undercuts the speaker and the *carpe diem* attitude he advocates.

Although he fully intends to go out into the woods, the speaker is basically inactive. Housman does not actually represent 'A walk though the woods at Eastertide' (Leggett, 'Insight' 329) or any other activity. Wherever the young man is in relation to the tree (the tree may exist only in his imagination, or it may be visible from the young man's window or door, or he may be outside standing next to it) is immaterial since he does not move from the spot where he lies, sits, or stands. His energetic call for action is vitiated by his present and obvious inaction. He does not act upon his expressed desire to experience as much beauty as he can (the plural and generalised 'things in bloom').

The speaker actually does only one thing: he composes or speaks or voices the poem. He discusses going for a walk, but he does not walk: his 'action' is sedentary. In addition, that he chooses just this moment to speak the poem undercuts what the poem says: the speaker calls for action and, as Perrine notes, the 'emphasis is on living life fully *now*' (27). 'Now' is emphasised by repetition, by position (at the end of one line and the beginning of another) and by being a stressed syllable and a rhyme word (Perrine 26). But in spite of that emphasis, the speaker composes or presents his poem (that is, he performs the one action of the poem) before or instead of setting out for his woodland ride. The disregard for the insistent 'now' of the first and second stanzas, and the postponement of action indicated by the switch to the future tense in the last stanza ('I will go') all contradict the sense of urgency the speaker claims to feel.

The sense of urgency is also undercut by the speaker's way of thinking. The speaker's represented thought processes are frustratingly slow: it takes him four lines, one third of the poem, to make a simple mathematical calculation that should be done instantaneously. Leggett defends this 'attention to arithmetic', claiming that it allows Housman to avoid 'the danger of a maudlin treatment of a commonplace experience by the neutrality of tone and attention to detail', much as Frost does by focusing on the horse and the owner of the woods in 'Stopping by Woods' ('Insight' 330). But whereas Frost gives us something to defuse the situation (if that is indeed what he is doing), Housman attenuates a simple mathematical activity and emphasises the slowness of the very speaker who is urging haste. ( ... )

'Loveliest of trees' says a lively active thing, but in a slow and motionless way. The speaker's inaction contradicts his enthusiasm for walking in the woods and experiencing beauty. His stepping to compose a poem and his care with arithmetic deny his urgency. Whether Housman intended it or not, the poem's smooth façade covers a fundamental and unresolved tension.

## WORKS CITED

Leggett, B.J., *Housman's Land of Lost Content: a Critical Study of* A Shropshire Lad. Knoxville: U.Tenn. P., 1970.

Leggett, B.J., 'The Poetry of Insight: Persona and Point of View in Housman.' *Victorian Poetry* 14 (1976): 325–39.

Perrine, Laurence, 'Housman's Snow: Literal or Metaphorical?,' *CFA Critic* 35.1 (1972): pp 26–7.

Ricks, Christopher, 'The Nature of Housman's Poetry,' *Essays in Criticism* 14 (1964): 268–84.

—Miriam B. Mandel, "Housman's 'Loveliest of Trees.'" *Housman Society Journal*, 14, 1988: pp. 66–68


## ARCHIE BURNETT ON HOUSMAN'S "LEVEL TONES"

[Archie Burnett is a scholar, author, and editor, and Co-director of the Editorial Institute at Boston University. He has edited the Oxford edition of *The Poems of A.E. Housman*, and a collection of Housman's letters. Burnett is also well known for his work on Milton. In this excerpt, Burnett discusses the level "tone" or composure in Housman's poetry, and how this works against the strong, if understated, emotional pull of the poems' subject matter.]

Housman well knew that a judicious classical restraint in form and phrase could work both psychologically and aesthetically, sublimating emotion and making it sublime. Consider, for example, the 'level tones' at the close of *Last Poems* VII:

> The lover and his lass
>   Beneath the hawthorn lying
> Have heard the soldiers pass,
>   And both are sighing.
>
> And down the distance they
>   With dying note and swelling
> Walk the resounding way
>   To the still dwelling.

How gentle they go into that goodnight! Syntactic linkages and line divisions coincide, structures are smoothly coordinate ('And both are sighing ... And down the distance'), and sounds are harmonious in alliteration, echo and rhyme. However, the 'level tones' preserve a superficial simplicity that contains deeper complexities, producing, as Housman often does, an Empsonian version of pastoral.[7] 'The lover and his lass' invokes the innocent pastoral of *As You Like It* V.iii.15 ('It was a lover and his lass') in a context that intimates its demise, and the 'sighing' of the lovers is laden with the sadness of mortality. The words 'Pass', 'dying' in 'dying note' and 'still' in 'the still dwelling' may be ominous; 'swelling' and 'resounding' may be exultant; and 'dying' and 'swelling' and 'resounding' and 'still' may be disturbingly paradoxical; but ominousness, exultation and disturbance are alike levelled by a consistency of tone and mood. In the notebook drafts, 'And down the distance they' replaced three other versions: 'And you with colours gay', 'And deep in distance they', 'And ever onward they'. Gaiety would obtrude, 'ever onward' would be too earnestly resolute; and 'deep in distance' would sacrifice both the foreboding of 'down the distance' and the surface unremarkableness of walking down to the dwelling. 'With dying note and swelling' replaced 'And martial music swelling', 'The quickstep faintly swelling', and 'With fainter music swelling': the literalism of 'martial' and 'fainter', and the intrusive liveliness of 'quickstep', were alike rejected for 'dying note and swelling', which is portentous, but not pompous: beneath the sombre overtones is the flatter statement that the military music alternates dying and swelling notes, crescendo and diminuendo. In a context where surface innocence blends with darker experience, the everyday insouciance of 'Walk' takes on uncommon dignity—'Run' or 'Stroll', say, would be unthinkable, and in the second notebook draft Housman cancelled 'Pace' and 'Tread'. 'Level tones' preserve that dignity until the soldiers, and by suggestion the lovers, reach the finally (and finely) placed 'still dwelling'. The whole poem, and the ending in particular, fulfils the function of poetry that Housman once expounded in a letter to his sister:

> The essential business of poetry, as it has been said, is to harmonise the sadness of the universe; and it is somehow more sustaining and healing than prose.[8]

Such a statement suggests strongly that Housman in his poetry is concerned not merely with honouring classical precedent or with achieving correctness and polish, but rather with the handling of emotion, which in turn means finding an appropriate tone. Tone in Housman's poetry has attracted considerable attention, notably from Cleanth Brooks, Christopher Ricks, Brian Rosebury and John Bayley.[9] 'Level tones' are of particular significance, however, and for the reason that they give expression to an emotional life that is often far from level. Though Housman's poetry contains a considerable range of tone, the power and distinction of many of the poems seem to me to derive from intense personal feeling presented with formal public decorum.

A *Shropshire Lad* XXXI is a notable manifestation:

> On Wenlock Edge the wood's in trouble;
>   His forest fleece the Wrekin heaves;
> The gale, it plies the saplings double,
>   And thick on Severn snow the leaves.
>
> 'Twould blow like this through holt and hanger
>   When Uricon the city stood:
> 'Tis the old wind in the old anger,
>   But then it threshed another wood.

Then, 'twas before my time, the Roman
    At yonder heaving hill would stare:
The blood that warms an English yeoman,
    The thoughts that hurt him, they were there.

There, like the wind through woods in riot,
    Through him the gale of life blew high;
The tree of man was never quiet:
    Then 'twas the Roman, now 'tis I.

The gale, it plies the saplings double,
    It blows so hard, 'twill soon be gone:
To-day the Roman and his trouble
    Are ashes under Uricon.

The violence of the gale is emphasized. Nature is relentlessly, hectically active: the Wrekin heaves the forest fleece, the gale plies the saplings double, the leaves snow thick on Severn, the wind in anger threshes the wood, the hill heaves, the wind riots. Verbs are starkly monosyllabic ('heaves', 'plies', 'snow', 'threshed') and tremors surge through the poem's pervasive alliteration and assonance: 'On Wenlock Edge the wood's in trouble'; 'His forest fleece the Wrekin heaves'. No doubt it was such turbulence that prompted Vaughan Williams to create an uninhibitedly violent musical setting. Housman's poem, however, is not a turbulent one. The stanza stays regular, and balanced structures further establish a controlled steadiness, in simple coordinations:

The gale, it plies the saplings double,
    And thick on Severn snow the leaves.

'Tis the old wind in the old anger,
    But then it threshed another wood

or in the syntax and rhythm of individual lines: ''Tis the old wind in the old anger', 'Then 'twas the Roman, now 'tis I', 'It blows so hard, 'twill soon be gone'. Repetitions abound: 'the wood's in trouble' is echoed by 'the Roman and his trouble', 'the Wrekin heaves' reverberates in 'yonder heaving hill', and two lines are identical: 'The gale, it plies the saplings double'. Single words also recur— 'Roman', 'Uricon', 'wood(s)', 'gale'—and further accentuate the contrast between past and present that underlies the poem's theme: 'where Uricon the city stood' becomes 'ashes under Uricon', 'then' becomes 'now', and the present tenses of the first and last verses alternate with the past tenses of the others.

It is possible to read the poem as protest or as elegy: such is its capacity to resolve its internal conflict between passion and resignation into a single complex attitude. The speaker can say 'The tree of man was never quiet', and say it quietly; or remark 'it blows so hard, 'twill soon be gone' in the same breath. Throughout, repetitions can seem soothing or aggressively insistent. The speaker does not sound world-weary: the poem harnesses too much energy for that. But neither is he clamorous or distraught: it is too composed for that. Emotion is recollected in tranquillity, but the emotion recollected is not tranquil: the poem achieves equanimity, not by denying the forces of disturbance, but by containing them. ( ... )

In poetry, speaking with restraint was a necessity for Housman, for reasons at once aesthetic, emotional and social. He was never one to write without control, in prose or in poetry, and the fastidiousness he brought to classical scholarship can be seen also in the extensive drafting and redrafting of poems in his notebooks. Sometimes, however, emotion breaks through, threatening the 'level tones':

> Shot? so quick, so clean an ending?
> Oh that was right, lad, that was brave:
> Yours was not an ill for mending,
> 'Twas best to take it to the grave.
>
> Oh you had forethought, you could reason,
> And saw your road and where it led,
> And early wise and brave in season
> Put the pistol to your head.
>
> Oh soon, and better so than later
> After long disgrace and scorn,
> You shot dead the household traitor,
> The soul that should not have been born.
>
> Right you guessed the rising morrow
> And scorned to tread the mire you must:

Dust's your wages, son of sorrow,
    But men may come to worse than dust.

Souls undone, undoing others,—
    Long time since the tale began.
You would not live to wrong your brothers:
    Oh lad, you died as fits a man.

Now to your grave shall friend and stranger
    With ruth and some with envy come:
Undishonoured, clear of danger
    Clean of guilt, pass hence and home.

Turn safe to rest, no dreams, no waking;
    And here, man, here's the wreath I've made:
'Tis not a gift that's worth the taking,
    But wear it and it will not fade.

The poem is probably the nearest Housman came in his lifetime to speaking out about homosexuality. It relates to the suicide on 6 August 1899 at the age of 19 of Henry Clarkson Maclean, a gentleman Cadet at the Royal Military Academy, Woolwich. In his copy of *A Shropshire Lad*, at poem XLIV, Housman kept a press cutting of the coroner's inquest into the suicide,[30] and the source of the cutting was independently identified by William White as *The Standard* of 10 August 1895.[31] ( ... )

J. M. Nosworthy justly concludes that Housman attributed Maclean's depression to 'a recognition of irresistible homosexual tendencies'.[32]

The opening question, 'Shot?', makes an explosive impact, and, like the three occurrences of 'Oh' in the first 12 lines ('Oh that was right ... Oh you had forethought ... Oh soon'), it announces a tone far from level. What sounds like callously hectoring sarcasm in the opening verse is sustained in the first three. Then, in the next two, it is moderated into what sounds more like unequivocal praise. In the last two verses, the 'level tones' of elegiac tribute restore public decorum. The poem is the means of achieving composure. The opening verses are markedly unstable in tone and in attitude, and represent Housman's jibing mockery of conventional public complacency and piety. A similar tone and attitude underlie 'If it chance your eye offend you, / Pluck it out, lad, and be sound' (*ASL*

XLV), 'Think no more, lad; laugh, be jolly: / Why should men make haste to die' (*ASL* XLIX), and the poem on Wilde (*AP* XVIII):

> 'Tis a shame to human nature, such a head of hair as his;
> In the good old time 'twas hanging for the colour that it is;
> Though hanging isn't bad enough and flaying would be fair
> For the nameless and abominable colour of his hair.
>
> (ll. 5–8)

Such tone, unsettled, or nettled, is a just counter-response to unsettling social attitudes. ( ... )

The capacity to absorb disturbance into decorum can be seen in the 'Epitaph on an Army of Mercenaries', where it is a measure of Housman's poetic power that he can rebuke indifference or smugness or contempt without raising his voice:

> These, in the day when heaven was falling,
>     The hour when earth's foundations fled,
> Followed their mercenary calling
>     And took their wages and are dead.
>
> Their shoulders held the sky suspended;
>     They stood, and earth's foundations stay;
> What God abandoned, these defended,
>     And saved the sum of things for pay. ( ... )

On the term 'mercenaries', Housman commented that 'it was not the German Emperor but the German people which called ours a mercenary army, as in fact it was and is.'[35] ( ... )

The power of the poem lies in its 'level tones', which are achieved by steady rhythm accentuated by parallelism and sound patterning, and, emphatically, by coordinations that resist differentiation: 'Followed their mercenary calling / And took their wages and are dead', 'They stood, and earth's foundations stay', 'What God abandoned, these defended, / And saved the sum of things for pay'. If the poem persuades, it does so by not seeming overtly persuasive: its starkly uncompromising challenge rejects all adjectives but 'mercenary', and there are no adverbs. Is there not a pressure to stress 'What God abandoned, these defended', as though it were a heroic climax? Yes, but the poem both resists and absorbs that pressure, calmly insisting on the balanced weightiness of plain statement: 'What God abandoned, these defended'. ( ... )

Nowhere in the eight lapidary lines is a potential change in attitude signalled by a change in tone: the poem asks us to accept its statements as neutrally true. It is a triumph of tonelessness, and prompts the reflection that what Enoch Powell said of Housman's textual scholarship can be applied to many of the poems:

> The severity of Housman's presentation was the severity not of passionlessness but of suppressed passion, passion for true poetry and passion for truthfulness.[46]

NOTES

7. See William Empson, *Some Versions of Pastoral* (London: Chatto & Windus, 1935; rptd 1986) pp. 22, 53.

8. *Letters*, ed. Maas, p. 141.

9. For Brooks and Ricks, see *A. E. Housman: A Collection of Critical Essays*, ed. Ricks (Englewood Cliffs, NJ: Prentice-Hall, 1968) pp. 62–84, 106–22. Brian Rosebury's 'The Three Disciplines of A. E. Housman's Poetry' is in *Victorian Poetry* 21.3 (Autumn 1983) 217–28, and John Bayley's *Housman's Poems* was published in 1992 (Oxford: Clarendon Press).

30. Laurence Housman, *A. E. H.* (1937) pp, 103–5.

31. *The American Book Collector* 10.2 (1959) 25–6.

32. *Notes and Queries* NS 17 (1970) 352.

35. To The Richards Press, 14 November 1927: *Letters*, ed. Maas, p. 255.

46. *Housman Society Journal* 1 (1974) 28.

> —Archie Burnett, "A.E. Housman's 'Level Tones.'" *A.E. Housman: A Reassessment*, Alan W. Holden and J. Roy Birch, eds. (London and New York: MacMillan and St. Martin's Press, 2000): pp. 2–5, 10–12, 15–17.

## KEITH JEBB ON HOUSMAN'S ALTER EGO, "TERENCE"

[Keith Jebb is a poet, freelance writer, and lecturer who teaches in London and Oxford. His publications include *A.E. Housman* (1992), as well as poems published in various print and on-line journals. In this excerpt, he expands upon the notion of divided subjectivity in this critique of Housman's personae. His discussion of Terence Hearsay, the speaker of these poems, provides an historical context as it delves into this character's complicated and sometimes indistinct relationship to Housman the poet.]

Housman's popular reputation as a poet is unusual in that it is based so much upon a single collection of short lyrics, *A Shropshire Lad*. It is possible that more people know the title of this book than know the name of its author; but how many could tell you the title of one of Thomas Hardy's original volumes, and how many slim volumes of verse from the late nineteenth century are still available, under separate covers, having never gone out of print? The phenomenon takes some explaining. How much is it due to the unity of the volume and its presentation of the world of Housman's Shropshire? How much might it be due to its author's own refusal, for the forty years he lived after its publication, to have it printed as anything but a separate volume? It might even have something to do with the title, suggested by Arthur Pollard to replace the rather less memorable *Poems by Terence Hearsay*. Perhaps the matter will become a little clearer if we look at two almost inseparable subjects—the poet's Shropshire, and Shropshire's poet.

The first thing to say about Housman's Shropshire is that it is not, and never was, the county on the Welsh border normally represented by that name. In fact it is as mythical as the Britain of Tennyson's *Idylls of the King*, or the pastoral setting of Sir Philip Sidney's *Arcadia*. It is not that the poet did not know Shropshire well, having never lived there, though he didn't; it is not even that he falsified the geography of the place to suit himself, though he did: it is more that in creating Shropshire he produced a stage, a little world on which to set in motion the characters, the emotions and the dramas that he needed to portray. What he produced is therefore much closer to Tolkien's Middle Earth, than the historically-rooted accuracy of Hardy's Wessex. ( ... )

There is a strange paradox enacted in *A Shropshire Lad*. In the first half of the book, which deals mainly with characters in the Shropshire setting itself, life on the land is something to be escaped from, or so it seems. There is drinking and football and love, for which the lovers in 'Bredon Hill' defy the routine church-going that is expected of them. And in a different order of escape there is the army, and death. But the second half of the book, when the central figure of the poems has left for London, presents Shropshire as "the land of lost content" the place of happiness and innocence, which can never be reclaimed; the true pastoral idyll, which it never represented before, being then a place of betrayal, crime and punishment. ( ... )

What unifies the volume, apart from the pastoral setting in Shropshire, is the difficult figure of Terence Hearsay, at once the fictional author of and principal persona in the poems themselves.

Terence has remained a very elusive figure for Housman critics. Apart from knowing that the volume was to be called 'Poems by Terence Hearsay,' the only other evidence for him is the penultimate poem, *ASL* LXII, ' " Terence, this is stupid stuff " ', a dialogue between Terence and a friend, one of only two poems that mention him by name, as the book stands. From this it appears clear that he is the poet responsible for the preceding verses and that he is, in fact, the 'Shropshire Lad.' Apart from this, we have Housman's own words on the matter, from his letter to Maurice Pollet: "The Shropshire Lad is an imaginary figure, with something of my temper and view of life. Very little in the book is biographical" (*P.&P.* p. 469). It is interesting that it has become quite common to see Terence as a simple rustic poet, producing poems that are essentially simple and naive, whose ironies and insights are the product of their other author, A.E. Housman, playing the role of ventriloquist or puppet-master. There are many problems with this approach. It necessarily complicates our reading of the poems, in that you have to separate the poet-persona from the true poet and place the second on a higher plane of perception; meanwhile the poems continuously refuse to let themselves be broken down into two distinct readings, the simple one for the rustic poet, and the more subtle one for Housman and us. Housman's irony tends to be too inherent in the structure of the poems to allow this kind of separation.

> They tolled the one bell only,
>     Groom there was none to see,
> The mourners followed after,
>     And so to church went she,
>     And would not wait for me.
>                 (*ASL* XXI, 'Bredon Hill')

I have read an interpretation of this poem, which has the rustic persona of the poem (Terence?) actually accusing his lover of a kind of unfaithfulness here, as if he thought she died to spite him, so 'unsophisticated' was he taken to be. It is not uncommon for literary people to assume country people are lacking in some of their emotional equipment. ( ... )

It seems much more sensible to me to view Terence as a kind of *alter ego* for Housman, endowed not only with something of his temper and view of life, but with his poetic talent as well. At times he presents himself as a character in a poem, as in *ASL* VIII 'Farewell to barn and stack and tree', where he is the silent receiver of his friend's confession to murder. At times he is totally invisible: *ASL* XLIV, the poem about the Woolwich Cadet, whilst not biographical as such, is a poem we can assume to be very close to Housman's heart, something written without Terence Hearsay in mind. Indeed, a lot of the volume appears to have been written without, or before, the idea of Terence. ( ... )

Just as some of *A Shropshire Lad* predates Terence, so a lot of *Last Poems* consists of poems written in 1894–5 and bearing clear marks of his presence, *LP* XXIII 'In the morning, in the morning', for example; although a later poem like *LP* XX 'The night is freezing fast' (1922) still sounds as if it belongs to the fictional poet, with its familiar use of the Christian name: "And chiefly I remember / How Dick would hate the cold". So the fact is that the majority of the poems in *A Shropshire Lad* were written after Housman had conceived of the idea of a rural *alter ego*. ( ... )

I think we have to imagine something of the freedom the creation of this poet-mask would have given Housman, both in his writing, and in placing what he wrote before the public. This freedom would be complemented by the freedoms he took in his recreation of Shropshire.

—Keith Jebb, *A.E. Housman* (Mid Glamorgen, England: 1992): pp. 73, 78–79, 80.

# HOUSMAN'S FIGURATIONS OF TIME, AND THE POETIC TRADITION

## CRITICAL ANALYSIS OF
## *A Shropshire Lad* 19 and 21

With its common elegiac phrasing and imagery—"shady night," "sill of shade"—as well as rhyming couplets, *A Shropshire Lad* 19 "To an Athlete Dying Young," is evocative of earlier eighteenth-century elegies, such as those of Collins and Gray. "The sense of an ending" (to borrow Frank Kermode's term) is everywhere in this poem; Housman's typical use of tetrameter shortens the line, and the quatrains of rhyming couplets help to achieve a sense of finality in every stanza.

The poem is interesting for the manner in which it mourns. Curiously, instead of lauding the athlete's accomplishments, it focuses on the fact that they will eventually be overcome by time, memory, and the victories of others. This poem is also significant for its extreme irony; it congratulates the athlete for dying young, for this means he will never live to experience defeat, disappointment, or the anonymity that may come with old age and the neglect of his early achievements. The threat of anonymity is reinforced by the way this lad is only identified to us "an athlete"—in a sense already anonymous—his honour on the field is the only identifying characteristic. Moreover, those "whom honour outran" have lived to see their names "die" in the community's memory long before they do. Death, however, is more likely to insure the memory of one who died so young, as well as of his achievements.

As a component of the imaginary Shropshire community Housman creates in *A Shropshire Lad*, the poem itself serves as a public "record." And in a doubly elegiac gesture, *Shropshire* 19 acknowledges the death of this athlete, while simultaneously elegizing a community's collective memory of the athlete's death. This young man, once carried through the busy town market-place, is now carried through "a stiller town"—the town churchyard. While the first two stanzas record a public experience of life and death, those following address these matters through the private thoughts of the poet. As the poem proceeds, these thoughts begin to reveal a very personal response. The celebration of dying young is a rather peculiar reaction. The poet is no mere bystander; he seems to have an emotional investment in the athlete's death. He does not want to see the athlete live to "see the record cut," his laurels wither, and his name "die." The poem reveals that this anonymous lad is an object of identification or even desire for the speaker. In this sense, the poem seems as much an ode to the athlete as to death itself.

The gradual and subtle shift in emotion, from a public elegiac discourse to a personal response, is confirmed in the final stanza. The athlete is now envisioned as a citizen of that "stiller town." An image of the mythic Classical underworld is evoked in the first two lines, in which the underworld is a populated community—in some ways not unlike that of the living. In this underworld, even the dead recognize and admire the achievements of the athlete: "And round that early-laurelled head / "Will flock to gaze the strengthless dead." The poet is not content to remain at the grave on the "sill of shade," but accompanies the athlete to his new home, placing himself among the admirers in this otherworld.

The speaker describes his own vision of the dead young man in the final lines, and these lines betray his personal affection and love for the athlete. Although the dead man is described as an object—"the head," "its curls"—the details in these lines are those produced by feeling, not objective vision. The athlete's curls are the only physical description we are given, and it comes in the penultimate line, as if the entire progress of the poem has been leading both the speaker and the reader to this point: the point of personal recognition. What lies "unwithered" on those curls is a crown of laurels—a signifier of victory and achievement in the masculine world—but here that garland is something delicate, "briefer than a girl's." This image of something fragile—and in terms of the athlete's demonstrations of strength and stamina, even effeminate—seems as descriptive of the speaker's private feeling for the athlete as it is descriptive of the nature of this athlete's life. The use of "girl" here to suggest delicacy also suggests a kind of sexual substitution, if we read the poet's feelings or desire for the athlete to be "inappropriate." The phrase "briefer than a girl's" also calls to mind the fragility and often short span of human life, whether in Housman's Shropshire, or in the traditional themes of the elegiac tradition.

*A Shropshire Lad* 21, "Bredon Hill," continues the elegiac thread that runs throughout *A Shropshire Lad*. This poem exhibits extreme control over emotion, yet its tightly-reined irony betrays the speaker's grief and personal feeling to a significant degree. The poem's narrative is reminiscent of other Housman poems, in that it describes past experience and presents a very different perspective on the present. In this poem, however, the speaker's present is represented only in the final stanza; everything that precedes it is in past-tense.

The bells mark time in this poem: sound is the single, enduring element that connects past to present, person to person, community to community in "Bredon Hill." The bells, ringing "in steeples far and near," create a commonality between the speaker, his "love," and all of the "good people" within earshot. In the first three stanzas, the bells are overheard by the speaker and his companion, but their sound marks the distance this couple has created between themselves and the rest of their community. The poet answers the bells in his own, unorthodox way—not by going to church, but with a kind of rejoinder: "'Oh peal upon our wedding, / And we will hear the chime'." In other words, the couple will at last answer the calling of the bells when the bells announce their union. It can be read as both an invocation and a mild taunt.

The time suddenly shifts from summer to winter in the fifth stanza; and there is no sound to mark the change, nor the lover's disappearance. This is remarkable, for in every other stanza, something makes noise: bells, larks, the poet's voice. The lover who "rose up so early / And stole out unbeknown" has died—we learn that in the following stanza. Her silent movement in the fifth stanza can be read as a metaphor for her death, or more literally as the cause of her unexpected death.

Notably, in the sixth stanza, the ringing that once echoed "Round both the shires" have been reduced to a single tolling bell. What should has been the celebratory peal of wedding bells becomes a funeral march. The sound of one bell here signifies both the occasion and the solitude of the speaker: "She would not wait for me." This solitude is elaborated on in the final stanza: The weekly calling to worship in Shropshire continues, despite the events in the speaker's own life. Bells that trace the continuity from past to present, now mark the alienation of the speaker from his community, and from his future hopes. His wish for silence—"Oh, noisy bells, be dumb"—constitutes a different kind of invocation. It can be read as his wish to break the continuity they represent, which is a break from the past. Yet the final line is ambiguous. The tone reveals impatience and resignation. But for what is he impatient? To what has the speaker resigned himself? It seems this can be read in two ways. "I hear you, I will come." The speaker has perhaps resigned himself to his loss and his alienation; although he may rejoin the community in presence, he cannot do so in spirit. There is a darker implication in this line, however, and this is the suggestion of the speaker's own death. It is not merely a premonition; the word "will" signifies both the future—that is, the inevitability of death—and a determination, on the speaker's part to achieve it. The line "I hear you, I will come" is laden with impatience, even spite: after all, the bells that have marked his hopes and his sorrows are inanimate objects, unaware of the human time they mark, and numb to human feeling. Yet the poet addresses them directly: in doing so, he acknowledges the futility of his own desire and perhaps even the futility of all desire in the face of time.

# CRITICAL VIEWS ON
# *A Shropshire Lad* 19 and 21

## HOLBROOK JACKSON ON HOUSMAN'S LYRICISM

[Holbrook Jackson (1874–1948) was an author and the editorial director of the National Trade Press, Ltd. He also edited *T.P.'s Weekly* and *Today*. Among his many publications is *The Eighteen Nineties* (1913), an intellectual history and review of art at the end of the nineteenth century. His essay on Housman is a general overview of themes in *A Shropshire Lad*; it also considers some of the lyrical and poetic resonances Housman's poetry has with other authors and works of literature.]

Incidentally, and surprisingly, taking into account Housman's scholarly life, many of the poems in 'A Shropshire Lad' move to the sound of bugles, and all of them are robust as a man of action rather than a scholar might understand robustness. Yet they have none of the staccato boisterousness which distinguishes the soldier-poems of Rudyard Kipling, or the traditional romanticism of the sailor-poems of Sir Henry Newbolt. I use the comparison not in disparagement of either Kipling or Newbolt, but by way of distinguishing one type of poetry from another. Housman is equally robust, or manly, if you like, but he brings deeper reflection to his theme, less apparent effort, and he is passionate where they are emotional. He does not depend for effect upon the heroics of splendid activity, but upon the meditative reactions of soldiering. For instance, let us take his moving lyric called 'The Recruit':

> Leave your home behind,
>     And reach your friends your hand,
> And go, and luck go with you
>     While Ludlow Tower shall stand.
>
> Oh, come you home of Sunday
>     When Ludlow streets are still
> And Ludlow bells are calling
>     To farm and lane and mill.

There, in brief lines and simple words, you have concentrated the feelings of those who lose a lad to soldiering, and they imply the feelings also of the recruit himself in association with home sights and sounds. But there is no mawkish regret. The pensive note is natural and universal. You find it also in the popular music-hall ballad, 'We don't want to lose you, but we think you ought to go,' put, of course, less poetically and less profoundly, but none the less truly. Nor does Housman reject the martial and patriotic appeal of soldiering:

> And you will list the bugle
> > That blows in lands of morn,
> And makes the foes of England
> > Be sorry you were born.

The patriot element of the poems does not depend for effect upon flags and trumpets. Cheers and tears companion one another, and such tumult as they have is inward, the beating of a humble and a contrite heart at the tragedy of patriotic heroism and sacrifice.

The two themes, tragedy and heroism, go hand in hand; not apart, as in false romance. Housman's soldier is brave in the great spirit. He does not go to war convinced that he will escape with his life; he goes to war convinced that he may lose his life, and, because it is necessary, he goes willingly, cheerfully, hoping for nothing but the good luck of good fortune.

Nor does the poet forget the more human accessories of soldiering. He does not separate his Shropshire lad from love and good cheer. You feel always that there is a girl lurking in the background with warm heart for the soldier lad, and, at the end of the day's march, a tankard of ale:

> The lads in their hundreds to Ludlow come in for the fair,
> > There's men from the barn and the forge and the mill and the fold;
> The lads for the girls and the lads for the liquor are there,
> > And there with the rest are the lads that will never be old.

And somewhere the soldier's thoughts go back to the girl he left behind him:

> Is my girl happy
> > That I thought hard to leave,
> And has she tired of weeping
> > As she lies down at eve?

You get glimpses of soldiers marching away, and of mothers' eyes and hearts following them, and you are given to understand that such things are hard to bear on both sides, as you always did understand, although you never tire of being reminded of it; and also that there are valiant hearts capable of facing and bearing such trials. In a beautiful lyric the quintessence of regret is revealed with a master's touch:

> With rue my heart is laden
>  For golden friends I had,
> For many a rose-lipt maiden
>  And many a lightfoot lad.

Some of Housman's lyrics have all the grace of the little songs of the Shakespearean era. ( ... )

One would imagine that the author of 'A Shropshire Lad' took the same view of death as Walt Whitman. Not so much that death is a benignant mother, welcoming all at length with open arms; although equally benignant, death for him is more in the nature of an impersonal fact steeped in the infinite wisdom of quietness. Since we needs must die some day, and since it is our nature to stave off that day as long as possible, it is on the whole wise to die. He is reconciled as the philosopher is reconciled:

> Yet down at last he lies
> And then the man is wise.

There is one poem in the little book in which the Housman point of view seems to have crystallized. The poet is upbraided by 'A Shropshire Lad' for his melancholy lay, and he is bidden to 'Pipe a tune to dance to,' and the implication is that beer is more exalting than such verse:

> Why, if 'tis dancing you would be
> There's brisker pipes than poetry
> Say, for what were hopyards meant,
> Or why was Burton built on Trent?
> Oh many a peer of England brews
> Livelier liquor than the Muse,
> And malt does more than Milton can
> To justify God's ways to man.
> Ale, man, ale's the stuff to drink
> For fellows whom it hurts to think:

> Look into the pewter pot
> To see the world as the world's not.

But actually the poet refuses to do so, for the reason that he is aware of the mischief following such proceedings. I do not know whether we are to take literally the poet's confession that he has often been to Ludlow Fair and left his necktie God knows where! I should say not. But I think we are justified in taking literally the following explanation of his own attitude to his own Muse:

> Therefore, since the world has still
> Much good, but much less good than ill,
> And while the sun and moon endure
> Luck's a chance, but trouble's sure,
> I'd face it as a wise man would,
> And train for ill and not for good.
> 'Tis true, the stuff I bring for sale
> Is not so brisk a brew as ale:
> Out of the stern that scored the hand
> I wrung it in a weary land.
> But take it; if the smack is sour,
> The better for the embittered hour;
> It should do good to heart and head
> When your soul is in my soul's stead;
> And I will friend you, if I may,
> In the dark and cloudy day.

People are frightened of the word pessimism, and the word optimism has become a folly and a weariness of the flesh. Nowadays it is tripped about the market-place like a vain thing, so that wise folk shun it. But one should beware of labels whatever they are. Actually there is no pessimism and less optimism. Those of us who are blessed with health of body and mind, and even those who have only health of mind, are impelled by instinct to be as happy as possible, so long as they are not thinking about their little or their great woes. Perhaps, after all, happiness that comes naturally is the only form of health, and the healthy person resents a spurious happiness whether in verse or laughter. Housman must be ranked amongst the happy poets because he is strong enough to look sorrow in the face.

Despite the eternal regret which Housman shares with the Book of Ecclesiastes, with Lucretius, with Omar, with Keats, his most restless lines burn with the bright stillness of Pater's gem-like flame. It is the stillness of depth and intensity; an English calm of manner reflecting balance and control of feeling. A.E. Housman is very English, and his sense of love reaches nearest to passion at thought of the English scene. Shropshire in all her pastoral loveliness lives in his verses and there is no shire more English despite its proximity to Wales. Whether he sings of noble Shrewsbury herself where

> The flag of morn in conqueror's state
> Enters at the English gate:
> The vanquished eve, as night prevails,
> Needs upon the road to Wales;

or Ludlow; or Teme or Borne or Severn, or 'the wild green hills of Wyre,' the Wrekin, or 'the high-reared head of Clee,' he catches and enchains in his art the colour and character of place and the love thereof. Generally he achieves his effects by the difficult way of simplicity. He has no tricks either of metre or manner. He sings in the great tradition. Sometimes he surprises by the fine excess of well-conceived imagery, but more often by excessive fineness of thought and feeling in fastidiously chosen and inevitably placed words of the simplest class. He is a poet apart from 'movements.' The decadence which saw the birth of 'A Shropshire Lad' passed it by. Housman was in it, but not of it. Whilst every young poet of the nineties was dipping his bucket into foreign and often not very clean wells, he was quaffing the undefiled waters of English song. Something of the spirit of folk-song, something of Elizabethan lyricism, something of peasant dialect song, but in normal language, and something of all that is sweet and strong and simple of the English poetry, which does not depend for attraction upon conceits or tricks, or need to experiment, because it is allied with a tradition which cannot die.

—Holbrook Jackson, "The Poetry of A.E. Housman." *Today V*, August 1919. Reprinted in *A.E. Housman: The Critical Heritage*, Philip Gardner, ed. (London and New York: Routledge, 1992): pp. 104–109.

# CLEANTH BROOKS ON HOUSMAN'S USE OF NEO-ROMANTICISM

[Cleanth Brooks, a prodigious and highly influential twentieth-century American critic, was Gray Professor of Rhetoric at Yale University. Among his most well known books is *The Well Wrought Urn*, a widely read work of "The New Criticism." This essay explores Housman's control of tone and the effects of "tonal shifts" in *A Shropshire Lad*.]

Sentimentality is a failure of tone. The emotion becomes mawkish and self-regarding. We feel that the poet himself has been taken in by his own sentiment, responds excessively, and expects us to respond with him in excess of what the situation calls for. And so the writer who, like Housman, insists so uniformly upon the pathos of loss, upon the imminence of death, and upon the grim and loveless blackness to come, must be adept at handling the matter of tone.

Housman's great successes (as well as his disastrous failures) are to be accounted for in terms of tone. It does not matter that Housman never himself employs the term. *We* need it, nevertheless, in order to deal with Housman's poetry: for control of tone is the difference between the shrill and falsetto and the quiet but resonant utterance; it is the difference between the merely arch and self-consciously cute and the full-timbred irony; it is the difference between the sentimental and the responsibly mature utterance. Housman's characteristic fault is a slipping off into sentimentality. (One may observe in passing that this is also Hemingway's characteristic fault.) Conversely, Housman's triumphs nearly always involve a brilliant handling of tone—often a startling shift in tone—in which the matter of the poem is suddenly seen in a new perspective.

"The night is freezing fast" exhibits the kind of tonal shift of which I am speaking. "The Immortal Part" will furnish an even clearer example. In this poem, the speaker perversely insists that the immortal part of man is his skeleton—not the spirit, not the soul—but the most earthy, the most nearly mineral part of his body. The bones will endure long after the "dust of thoughts" has at last been laid and the flesh itself has become dust.

The device on which the poem is built is the grumbling complaint of the bones. The speaker begins by telling us that he can hear his bones counting the days of their servitude and predicting the day of their deliverance in which the flesh will fall away from them and leave them free and unfettered. Housman allows to the bones a certain lugubrious eloquence.

> "Wanderers eastward, wanderers west,
> Know you why you cannot rest?
> 'Tis that every mother's son
> Travails with a skeleton.

The reference to "wanderers" makes one suppose that "travails" is spelled "travels," but in fact the word is "travails"; and this suggestion of the travail of childbirth is developed fully in the next two stanzas:

> "Lie down in the bed of dust;
> Bear the fruit that bear you must;
> Bring the eternal seed to light,
> And morn is all the same as night.
>
> "Rest you so from trouble sore,
> Fear the heat o' the sun no more,
> Nor the snowing winter wild,
> Now you labour not with child.
>
> "Empty vessel, garment cast,
> We that wore you long shall last.
> —Another night, another day."
> So my bones *within me* say.

The colloquy of the bones is brilliant. But can the brilliance be indefinitely sustained? After nine stanzas, there is every danger of monotony. What climatic threat is there left for the bones to utter? And if there is none, how end the poem?

What Housman does is to introduce a brilliant shift in tone. The man answers back:

> Therefore they shall do my will
> To-day while I am master still,
> And flesh and soul, now both are strong,
> Shall hale the sullen slaves along,
>
> Before this fire of sense decay,
> This smoke of thought blow clean away,
> And leave with ancient night alone
> The stedfast and enduring bone.

But this defiance of the bones implies in fact a conviction of the truth of their ultimate triumph. Indeed, the "I" who speaks concede's the bones' eventual victory, and furthermore the last four lines of his speech of defiance simply turn into an echo of the chant of the bones. But the tone of the poem has shifted: the conscious sentient being has refused to collapse before the certain onslaught of time. The human spirit is given its due. The worst has been faced and faced down, though not denied.

Housman's use of a shift in tone is so important in his poetry generally that I should like to exhibit still another instance—one of Housman's finest, that which he employs in "Bredon Hill."

The lovers on many a Sunday morning on Bredon Hill have listened to the church bells ringing out through the valleys.

> In summertime on Bredon
>   The bells they sound so clear;
> Round both the shires they ring them
>   In steeples far and near,
>   A happy noise to hear.
>
> Here of a Sunday morning
>   My love and I would lie,
> And see the coloured counties,
>   And hear the larks so high
>   About us in the sky.

In their own happiness the lovers would put words to the sound of the bells:

> The bells would ring to call her
>   In valleys miles away:
> "Come all to church, good people;
>   Good people, come and pray."
>   But here my love would stay.
>
> And I would turn and answer
>   Among the springing thyme,
> "Oh, peal upon our wedding,
>   And we will hear the chime,
>   And come to church in time."

But his sweetheart comes to church before their time.

But when the snows at Christmas
    On Bredon top were strown,
My love rose up so early
    And stole out unbeknown
    And went to church alone.

They tolled the one bell only,
    Groom there was none to see,
The mourners followed after,
    And so to church went she,
    And would not wait for me. ( ... )

I think that you can "hear" the shift in tone as I read this last stanza:

The bells they sound on Bredon,
    And still the steeples hum.
"Come all to church, good people,"—
    Oh, noisy bells, be dumb;
    I hear you, I will come.

The note of exasperation—the irritated outburst against the noise of the bells—is a powerful, if indirect way, of voicing the speaker's sense of loss. All come to death; he will come to the churchyard too; but now that his sweetheart has been stolen from him, what does it matter *when* he comes. The bells whose sound was once a happy noise to hear have become a needless and distracting noisiness. The lover shuts them up as he might the disturbing prattle of a child:

Oh, noisy bells, be dumb;
I hear you, I will come.

—Cleanth Brooks, "Alfred Edward Housman." *A.E. Housman: A Collection of Critical Essays*, Christopher Ricks, ed. (Englewood Cliffs, NJ: Prentice-Hall, Inc., 1968): pp. 69–73

## R.L. KOWALCZYK ON THE CLASSICAL TRADITION IN HOUSMAN'S POETRY

[R.L. Kowalczyk, a critic and, at the time of this essay's publication, Professor at the University of Detroit, discusses Housman's employment of Classical Greek pastoral tradition in *A Shropshire Lad*.]

The nature of Housman's poetic vision in *A Shropshire Lad* has caused continuous scholarly debate since his death in 1936. His lyrics have been classified either as pessimistic for their denial of supernatural truths or as romantic for their cultivation of sentiment, either as decadent for their seemingly aimless and contradictory standards or as Georgian for their dependence upon the artificialities of the pastoral world. Scholarly opinion is further led into a labyrinth by vague agreement that Housman is classical only in style and technique. Aside from divorcing form from matter, this latter view of Housman places his poetic reputation in jeopardy and obscures his relationship to the Victorian scene. Abused as having very little to say and as being repetitiously sentimental, Housman's poetry is dismissed as "minor poetry well expressed." Furthermore, biographical or psychological perspectives have so obscured Housman's contribution to literature that the time has come, and is indeed long overdue, for an assessment not distorted by these perspectives.

I might be laboring an obvious point to suggest that Housman the classical scholar and Housman the poet, recognized as classical in technique, are not to be separated, as for example, scholars tend to separate Coleridge the poet and Coleridge the versifier; nevertheless, Housman's poetry has been subject to attack precisely because critics fail to see the connection between his classicism (both in attitude and theme) and his display of poetic techniques reminiscent of the Latin poets. The damaging attacks upon Housman as witless and sentimental stem from a misunderstanding of his purpose in creating his Shropshire world. It is my intention to survey the environs of his Shropshire as an emanation of the classical, pastoral world which the poet sees as a dramatic myth for conveying his poetic vision of man as a minute, but tragically honorable, particle in the impersonal universe. ( ... )

Correlative to Housman's basic denial of supernatural truth is his conception of the impersonal nature of the world and the fated existence of man. His poems, which directly deny supernatural order, indirectly reflect upon the status of man,[3] but in *A Shropshire Lad* his beliefs concerning the role of man divorced from the security of absolute, supernatural truths are expressed with the restraint and impersonalism of the classics. Housman's Shropshire mirrors through its mythical connotations the turmoil and pain of man's existence, the burdens of human nature which Catullus calls universal:

suus cuique attributus est error:  
sed non videmus manticae quod in tergost.　　(xxii, 20-21)[4]

In the Shropshire cycle Housman creates the persona, the melancholy, mad Terence Hearsay, who voices man's conception of *summa rerum*, the irrevocable cycle of change and man's philosophical resignation or violent reaction to the inevitable force of evil in life. These themes comprise the central position of a poetic tradition which scholars tend to relate only to the poet's style or diction. An understanding of Housman's classical spirit will then reveal his relationship to other Victorian poets, Tennyson, Landor, Arnold, Stevenson, Hardy, who worked in the pastoral mode.

An understanding of Housman's fear of and his concern for the demands of time are necessary for perceiving the nature of his mythical world. He transforms the classical, pastoral setting into its modern counterpart, Shropshire. The difference between the pastoral world of escape and the vicious Shropshire of his poems provides the tension with which he expresses the general decline of order in the world.

The dominating attitude by which Housman manifests his pastoral world is not one envisioning Shropshire as a land of escape nor as a land of the dead.[5] Shropshire is too violent for the one, and too vital for the other. The Shropshire inhabitants, with whom Housman identifies himself along with all men, are impregnated with the sense of time's swiftness which conditions their hollow attempts to bring some meaning to their brief and discontented lives.[6] Their actions are the frantic efforts of men to ward off the advance of old age and to preserve youthful vitality in the war against deterioration and death. At birth they find themselves judged and condemned by time to one destiny in death. While Terence, Housman's mask, notes the impersonal relationship between man and the natural background of his alluring pastoral world, he also sees a correlation between nature's unchanging cycles and the laws of mutability to which men are subjected.[7] Man's brief life-span, to Housman, also follows an unchanging flow, from birth and the passions of youth, to the deterioration of man's powers in old age and their obliteration in the finality of death. Housman dramatizes his concern for this fated judgment of man behind the mask of Terence in *A Shropshire Lad*, thus permitting himself escape from critical anathema while giving his view intensity through its depersonalization.

The fervent activity and violence of Housman's mythical world may then be explained in terms of man's reaction to a phenomenological interpretation of the world as articulated philosophically by Lucretius and poetically by the Latin elegists, as in Horace's ode:

> fugit retro
> levis iuventas et decor, arida
> pellente lascivos amores
> canitie facilemque somnum.
>
> non semper idem floribus est honor
> vernis, neque uno luna rubens nitet
> voltu: quid aeternis minorem
> consiliis animum. fatigas? (II, xi, 5–12)[8]

There is no wisdom in the view that men should ignore their impending doom. For both the elegists and Housman, discernment of time's swiftness is the inspiration for the creation of a pastoral world which permits them the license to express sentiment through their rustic and simple protagonists, as well as the possibility to present for acceptance alternate systems of value, Stoicism and Epicureanism. The major emphasis on the laws of mutability also partially explains the classical spirit of the elegists who rebelled against the notion of supernatural benevolence. ( ... )

The acceptance of mutability as the basic pattern of life in Shropshire suggests why Housman expresses his fear of old age and his longing for a cherished and unchanging past. Terence's concern in "To an Athlete Dying Young" is to remark that the youth has died before his honors fade, and by extension, before his youthful senses and prowess deteriorate. [ ... ] Terence's estimate focuses upon the realization that man is the product of an impersonal fate which places him in a world in which be feels insignificant. ( ... )

Just as the townsfolk cheered the victorious runner as they carried him triumphantly through the marketplace, Terence acclaims the youth as a greater champion when all tongues are struck dumb during his funeral procession. To the poet, the athlete is not merely a long-distance runner, but rather a man who outstrips the common lot of man. To his closed eyes the record stands, his prowess is honored, and his fame is unfleeting:

Now you will not swell the rout
Of lads that wore their honours out,
Runners whom renown outran
And the name died before the man.                    (*SL*, xix)

The theme, that those who die before their honors fade, before they experience the deadening of their senses and other physical or mental harbingers of old age, are truly fortunate, obtains dramatic poignancy, since the rustic poet has succeeded in finding and identifying a selected champion and exception to time's law. Such is not the case in *A Shropshire Lad*, XXIII, "The lads in their hundreds to Ludlow come in for the fair," where Housman reverses his technique. Here he does not select a youth of extraordinary calibre to investigate further extensions of the lad's strength and ability; instead, he bypasses exterior characteristics with a procession of numerous rustics to suggest that there are among the group of boisterous lads some truly fortunate ones "that will never grow old." The futility of Terence's search to discern an unidentifiable and unpredictable feature of man's fortunes again mirrors the futility of man's effort to escape the taint and smear of corruption:

But now you may stare as you like and there's nothing to scan;
And brushing your elbow unguessed-at and not to be told
They carry back bright to the coiner the mintage of man,
The lads that will die in their glory and never be old.

When cast into the illusory, pastoral world the "fortunate" lads, who must pay for their distinction by the oblivion of death, emerge as heroes unlike most men who face death as common representatives of humanity, soiled by sorrow and suffering, and weakened by the ravages of time—when their nature is the decayed shell of their former vitality.

The sense of time, hanging threateningly over Shropshire's inhabitants, places the pastoral world with its passivity, escape, and idealism into a new framework.

NOTES

3. *SL*, I, XLVIII. This theme occurs frequently in Housman's works, as *LP*, XII; *MP*, I, II, XIII. *AP*, XXI. I have used throughout these notes the following abbreviations: *SL*, *A Shropshire Lad*; *LP*, *Last Poems*; *MP*, *More Poems*; and *AP*,

*Additional Poems.* All quotations are from *The Complete Poems of A. E. Housman,* Centennial Edition, ed. Tom Burns Haber (New York, 1959).

4. "Everybody has his own delusion assigned to him: but we do not see that part of the bag which hangs on our back." (See also Tibullus, I, V, 3–4; II, IV, 11–12.)

5. John Peale Bishop, "The Poetry of A. E. Housman," *Poetry,* LVI (1940), 151–152. Most critics agree that Shropshire is a pastoral world and take it to mean a land of romantic escape. George Rylands sees the lads as corresponding to Thestylis and Corydon of the artificial pastoral in *Words and Poetry* (London, 1928), p. 53. Others holding the same position are Stephen Gwynn, "The Poetry of Mr. A. E. Housman," *DR,* III (1924) 435. Clement Wood, "The Shropshire Corydon: Opus II," *Nation,* CXVI (February 21, 1923), 22–23; H. W. Garrod takes Housman's pastoralism as his chief object of attack in *The Profession of Poetry* (Oxford, 1929), p. 223; Neville Watts takes the same approach in "The Poetry of A. E. Housman," *DubR,* CC (1937), 118. Louis MacNeice expressed the modern view in seeing Shropshire as an imaginary country for the purposes of personal mythology. See his *The Poetry of W. B. Yeats* (New York, 1941), pp. 78–79. One of the most perceptive studies of Housman in the tradition of the pastoral elegy is Michael Macklem's "The Elegiac Theme in Housman," *QQ,* LIX (1952), 39–52.

6. Elizabeth Drew in *Discovering Poetry* (New York, 1933), pp. 5–6, comments that Housman used the pastoral in the manner of Marvell for meditation on man's discontents.

7. Horace expresses this conception succinctly—"pulvis et umbra sumus ... " (IV, vii, 16)—and with cogency in a poem which Housman translates. This translation also emphasizes man's swift mortality:

> The swift hour and the brief prime of the year
>     Say to the soul, Thou wast not born for aye.
> Thaw follows frost; hard on the heel of spring
>     Treads summer sure to die, for hard on hers
> Comes autumn, with his apples scattering;
>     Then back to wintertide, when nothing stirs.          (*MP,* v)

8. Fresh youth and beauty are speeding fast away behind us, while wizened age is banishing sportive love and slumbers soft. Not for ever do the flowers of spring retain their glory, nor does blushing Luna shine always with the selfsame face. Why, with planning for the future, weary thy soul unequal to the task?"

—R.L. Kowalczyk, "Horatian Tradition and Pastoral Mode in Housman's *A Shropshire Lad." Victorian Poetry* IV: 4, 1966: pp. 223, 224–226, 227–228.

# B.J. Leggett on Housman's "Songs of Innocence and Experience"

[B.J. Leggett is Distinguished Professor of Humanities at the University of Tennessee. He has published two books and numerous articles on Housman, as well as works on Wallace Stevens. This essay, taken from his book *The Poetic Art of A.E. Housman,* uses William Blake's eighteenth-century *Songs of Innocence and Experience* as a metaphor through which to read the dichotomies and definition of "innocence" and "experience" in Housman's work.]

A large number of the poems of *A Shropshire Lad* deal directly with the moment of insight and exhibit a progressive structure which carries the persona from innocence to knowledge or from expectation to disillusionment. Most of these are found in the first half of *A Shropshire Lad,* which concentrates on the innocent's encounter with the alien world of death and change. In the last half of *A Shropshire Lad,* in *Last Poems,* and to some extent in the posthumous collections are found the lyrics which depend for their effect on the persona's recognition of the gulf which lies between innocence and experience and on his reaction to his exiled state. The structural patterns here are more varied because the feelings of the persona have acquired an ambivalence missing in the poems of the first group. ( ... )

The progressive pattern of imagery is one means of communicating a shift in perspective without the necessity of having the persona articulate his own understanding of the process of change he is undergoing, and it is made necessary by the essentially inarticulate nature of Housman's persona. The device is used successfully in "Bredon Hill," where the bells heard by the young lovers as wedding bells in springtime become funeral bells in winter, a structural pattern which parallels the color imagery of "Loveliest of Trees." The structure of "Bredon Hill" is more complex, however, since the speaker continues the wedding image in describing his love's death:

But when the snows at Christmas
   On Bredon top were strown,
My love rose up so early
   And stole out unbeknown
   And went to church alone.

They tolled the one bell only,
   Groom there was none to see,
The mourners followed after,
   And so to church went she,
   And would not wait for me.
               [ll. 21–30]

As does "Loveliest of Trees," the poem conveys a sense of the persona's discovery of human transience which he is himself incapable of describing. He views the girl's death as if it were an act of conscious will, as if he has been betrayed by his lover, who "stole out unbeknown," to meet another suitor.[4] The conception of human transience which this poem conveys thus comes not so much through the persona's understanding as through the reader's interpretation of the speaker's more limited point of view. The persona's own sense of loss and his awareness, at the end of the poem, that the innocence and permanence of young love were illusory, are voiced in an almost childish manner:

The bells they sound on Bredon,
   And still the steeples hum.
'Come all to church, good people,'—
   Oh, noisy bells, be dumb;
   I hear you, I will come.
              [ll. 31–35]

The last line indicates that he is now aware that he too must follow his love to church. The bells now toll only a song of death, but his perception is conveyed in a tone of childish petulance: "Oh, noisy bells, be dumb." These are the bells described in the first stanza as "A happy noise to hear," and it is through the shifts in the poem's imagery and the modulations in tone as the poem develops that the final two lines achieve their power.

It is, indeed, through the structural devices of his poetry that Housman is enabled so frequently to invest the commonplace observations of his persona with some significance. ( ... )

One sometimes has the impression that the poems of the type discussed here exist only for that moment when the persona utters the equivalent of "Oh, 'tis true," whether it is the resolve to watch the cherry hung with snow or the words spoken to the funeral bells, "I hear you, I will come." In "On Wenlock Edge" that moment is contained in the line "Then 'twas the Roman, now 'tis I," which serves to bring the separate strands of the poem together. The structure of "On Wenlock Edge" has been examined in some detail by Spiro Peterson,[5] who notes that the poem is built on two dominant motifs. The first is the historical perspective of man as represented by the comparison of the English yeoman who now watches the storm on Wenlock Edge and the Roman he imagines as having observed the same scene when the hill was the site of the Roman city Uricon. The second motif, which parallels the first, is suggested primarily by the poem's imagery, and it involves the further correlation between man and nature. Both patterns are set out in the opening stanzas:

> On Wenlock Edge the wood's in trouble;
> His forest fleece the Wrekin heaves;
> The gale, it plies the saplings double,
> And thick on Severn snow the leaves.
>
> 'Twould blow like this through holt and hanger
> When Uricon the city stood:
> 'Tis the old wind in the old anger,
> But then it threshed another wood.
>
> Then, 'twas before my time, the Roman
> At yonder heaving hill would stare:
> The blood that warms an English yeoman,
> The thoughts that hurt him, they were there.
>
> [ll. 1–12]

The yeoman's description of the natural setting, with the woods "in trouble" because of the wind's "old anger," carries the implication that nature reflects the plight of man. This correlation is strengthened in stanza 4 with the metaphors of "gale of life" and "tree of man." It is more than the conventional pathetic fallacy of nature poetry, for the speaker sees that, literally, man and nature are subject to the same life force. This force, which is represented by the wind, also serves to universalize the theme by linking Englishman and Roman, present and past. The first movement of the poem is thus a kind of expansion in which the private feelings of the persona are extended beyond himself in two directions—toward nature and back into the past. The movement serves as an escape from the privacy of the "thoughts that hurt him," but it is followed in stanza 4 by a contraction which brings the focus back to the speaker, though now with a new perspective:

> There, like the wind through woods in riot,
> Through him the gale of life blew high;
> The tree of man was never quiet:
> Then 'twas the Roman, now 'tis I.
> [ll. 13–16]

The studied understatement of the last line does not completely hide the persona's realization of the complex relationship of past and present, the generic plight of man and his own personal plight. The line suggests two conflicting moods, for it says both that his is a condition that all men must undergo and, conversely, that it is only in time, in the existing present, that the thoughts and feelings which trouble him have any significance. As in so many other Housman poems, the immediacy of feeling prevails finally, but the strategy of the poem's structure provides the necessary context in which the feelings are given meaning. It is curious that the poem ultimately implies the opposite of what it seems to be saying. It deals superficially with the universal subjugation of man and nature to a common fate, but its focus is on individual man, whose sense of that fate is what really matters to Housman. The final stanza extends the perspective of man and nature to the future in an indirect manner:

> The gale, it plies the saplings double,
> It blows so hard, 'twill soon be gone:
> To-day the Roman and his trouble
> Are ashes under Uricon.
> [ll. 17–20]

The storm will blow itself out, and to complete the parallel, the last two lines should be addressed to the speaker's future—soon he will be ashes under Uricon.[6] That is the sense of the poem's ending, but Housman again avoids a possibly maudlin conclusion by having the speaker project his own fate in terms of the impersonal past. It is an ambiguous ending. Is it comforting or painful to think that "then 'twas the Roman, now 'tis I"? The two moods are so mixed as to be indistinguishable. The focus of the poem is not on the speaker's reaction to his fate so much as on his realization of it. The triumph of the poem consists in the control of mood and tone, which are maintained through the concentration on the parallels of past and present, man and nature. In only one line of the poem are the speaker's feelings turned inward, yet the sense of his emotional turmoil and his contradictory passive acceptance of his brief role in the long process of generation is carried through the motifs of the troubled wood and the imaginary Roman bind his trouble, now "ashes under Uricon." ( ... )

A more successful instance of a structural pattern which depends on the shifts in tone signalled by the repetition and modulation of a refrain line is in the opening poem of *A Shropshire Lad*, "1887." As is true of many of the early poems of *A Shropshire Lad*, the tone of the poem shifts from an early mood of celebration to a final recognition of some element which qualifies or destroys it. The note of celebration is reflected in the first two stanzas by the festive atmosphere surrounding the commemoration of Victoria's Golden jubilee:

> From Clee to heaven the beacon burns,
>    The shires have seen it plain,
> From north and south the sign returns
>    And beacons burn again.
>
> Look left, look right, the hills are bright,
>    The dales are light between,
> Because 'tis fifty years to-night
>    That God has saved the Queen.
>                                   [ll. 1–8]

Housman's use of variations on the phrase "God save the Queen" carries with it overtones of the traditional, unthinking attitude toward God and country assumed on such occasions. The development of the theme of "1887" depends, however, on the way in which the poem redefines the traditional phrase. In the second and third stanzas it is associated with the dead soldiers, "friends of ours / Who shared the work with God" (ll. 11–12). This association leads to an identification of the soldiers with Christ, since they perished to save others, and the persona speaks of them in terms which recall the mocking of Christ in New Testament accounts: "The saviours come not home to-night: / Themselves they could not save" (ll. 15–16). The term save has, of course, undergone an important transformation, being shifted from its theological sense to mean simply "preserve" or "maintain," and that is the direction in which the poem moves—from an innocent faith in the operation of some unseen benevolent power to a recognition that the generic permanence of man rests on the transience of individual man. The last two stanzas of the poem bring this progression to its final stage:

> 'God save the Queen' we living sing,
>     From height to height 'tis heard;
> And with the rest your voices ring,
>     Lads of the Fifty-third.
>
> Oh, God will save her, fear you not:
>     Be you the men you've been,
> Get you the sons your fathers got,
>     And God will save the Queen.
>         [ll. 25–32]

The poem has been the subject of some critical controversy, which has centered on its tone. How are we to regard the apparently ironic treatment of a traditional, almost sacrosanct attitude? Housman denied that he was mocking the patriotism expressed in the poem,[9] and I am inclined to accept his statement at face value. The tone betrays no trace of sarcasm, and the function of Housman's redefinition of the phrase which expresses that patriotism is not mockery but the revelation of his persona's insight into the human condition in which patriotism finds its real meaning. The structure of the poem involves a process of revelation, and the repetition of the cant phrase in its different contexts carries the shifts in tone which reveal the growing insight of the persona. Shifting the burden of salvation from God to man does not lessen the speaker's admiration for the heroism involved in "saving" the queen, nor do I find the bitterness in his attitude which some commentators have noted. The final attitude is rather one of a recognition that the celebration of life is built on the foundation of death, a mood expressed so well in "Loveliest of Trees" when the persona resolves, after his sudden sense of mortality, to view the cherry, "hung with snow." The religious imagery of "1887" works in much the same manner as the nature imagery of "Loveliest of Trees." In both instances the structural development is dramatic, since its function is to capture the moment when the persona becomes aware of what is, for Housman, the most essential element of his consciousness. "1887" stands as the archetype of one of the most persistent structural patterns in Housman's poetry, though it is confined primarily to the first half of *A Shropshire Lad*.

The other pattern of development which influences most directly the shape of Housman's poetry begins to make its appearance in the second half of *A Shropshire Lad*, and it occurs frequently throughout the remainder of the collected poems. It depends heavily on the situation which Dylan Thomas exploits so well in lyrics like "Fern Hill"—the persona who remembers how it was to have been young and who captures in his memory of a blighted Eden the joy and pain of innocence as well as the gulf which now lies between him and his youth. In *A Shropshire Lad* this mood is signalled by the exile from the home shire and usually arises in the contrast between the Shropshire imagery, which recalls the state of innocence, and that implying the speaker's present exile:

> Into my heart an air that kills
>     From you far country blows:
> What are those blue remembered hills,
>     What spires, what farms are those?
>
> That is the land of lost content,
>     I see it shining plain,
> The happy highways where I went
>     And cannot come again.
>                     [*A Shropshire Lad* XL][10]

The prevailing mood of *Last Poems* is that of the second half of *A Shropshire Lad*, where the persona muses on his Shropshire youth from a new vantage point and sees both the loss and gain involved in the process of change. ( ... )

Housman most successfully evokes a sense of the lost past through his nature imagery. In *Last Poems* XL, "Tell me not here, it needs not saying," nature, embodied in the changing seasons, is an enchantress who beguiled the young man into thinking she was his:

> Tell me not here, it needs not saying,
>     What tune the enchantress plays

In aftermaths of soft September
    Or under blanching mays,
For she and I were long acquainted
    And I knew all her ways.
                    [ll. 1–6]

The tone is that of a love poem, and the lost sense of possessing nature is carried by sexual imagery. The point of view is that of the lover who looks back on a youthful affair from the vantage point of experience. He sees now that she was heartless and fickle, but he once possessed her. As in "The First of May," the mood is complicated by a blend of nostalgia for something beautiful which has been lost and the scornful attitude of maturity which belittles his earlier naiveté. The hint of sexuality pervades even the descriptions of seasonal change:

On acres of the seeded grasses
    The changing burnish heaves;
Or marshalled under moons of harvest
    Stand still all night the sheaves;
Or beeches strip in storms for winter
    And stain the wind with leaves.

Possess, as I possessed a season,
    The countries I resign,
Where over elmy plains the highway
    Would mount the hills and shine,
And full of shade the pillared forest
    Would murmur and be mine.
                    [ll. 13–24]

In the final stanza the sexual imagery is made explicit. Nature is a harlot who wantonly bestows her favors on whatever stranger chances to encounter her. She is not merely heartless, she is witless; it is only the innocent, ignorant of the character of nature's mindlessness, who could believe he possessed her:

For nature, heartless, witless nature,
    Will neither care nor know
What stranger's feet may find the meadow
    And trespass there and go,
Nor ask amid the dews of morning
    If they are mine or no.
                    [ll. 25–30]

Yet the young man did possess her, and the poem builds on the tension between the worlds of innocence and knowledge, both equally real. The later viewpoint does not cancel the former; it merely renders it more poignant. The disillusioned attitude of the world of knowledge controls the point of view, but the tone and imagery evoke the lost world of the adolescent. Although the speaker protests "it needs not saying," the tune the enchantress plays still beguiles him, and her music dominates the mood of the poem. It is a pattern—the simultaneous presentation of two conflicting moods—which Housman employs frequently in *Last Poems*.

## NOTES

4. As Cleanth Brooks notes in "Alfred Edward Housman," pp. 72–73. I am indebted to Brooks's reading of the poem.

5. "Housman's 'On Wenlock Edge,'" *Explicator* 15 (1956–57), Item 46.

6. As Peterson notes, the "sense of the complete parallel, the logic of the poem, the structure of the stanza demand the poem conclude with the same three words.... All the more conspicuous for their absence are the expected words, 'now 'tis I.'"

9. See Brooks, "Alfred Edward Housman," p. 76.

10. See Chapter 7, "The Exile Poems," in *Housman's Land of Lost Content*, pp. 108–130.

—B.J. Leggett, *The Poetic Art of A.E. Housman: Theory and Practice*. (Lincoln: University of Nebraska Press, 1978): pp. 63–65, 66–69, 70–73, 75–76.

# HOUSMAN IN THE VICTORIAN CONTEXT

## *Last Poems* 12, 34 and 40

Housman was known to be a curmudgeon, an atheist, and was a long-suspected "closeted" homosexual (unlike his brother Laurence, who made no secret of his homosexuality). *Last Poems* 12 ("The laws of God, the laws of man,") is uncharacteristically frank, and difficult not to read biographically, for it presents Housman's direct repudiation of Christianity and accepted social custom, as well as the British laws against sodomy. The incantatory style of this poem—tetrameter in rhyming couplets—ironically recalls the chant-like responsories of the church service. Yet its steadfast measure is, as well, a firm denial of the Judeo-Christian "laws of God and man." These laws, socially constructed as "natural," are claimed by the poet to be completely arbitrary. This does not detract from their power, however, and the poet's bitterness is everywhere apparent:

> ... make me dance as they desire
> With jail and gallows and hell-fire.
> And how am I to face the odds
> Of man's bedevilment and God's?

Cynicism, even glibness, in the face of such odds betray the speaker's anger and frustration: there is no choice but to submit. Housman's typically spare but precise, tightly-woven verse is employed in a rather facile manner here:

> Their deeds I judge and much condemn,
> Yet when did I make laws for them?
> Please yourselves, say I, and they
> Need only look the other way.

This predictable meter, syntax, and rather pat language is, perhaps, a response to the equally simple-minded and rigid nature of the people he describes here. There is no such thing as "live and let live" in the poet's world. In response, he declaims against and distances himself from the law. However, in doing so he must also alienate himself from society: "I, a stranger and afraid / In a world I never made."

*Last Poems* 12 elaborates on a theme of "social institutions and custom versus the individual," reiterating a familiar stance of personal alienation in Housman's work. However, this poem presents an untenable situation, for the poet must continue to live in the society that binds him. Thus, *Last Poems* 12 is a true poem of protest. Civil society is created by these laws of God and man, and although "both are foolish, both are strong"; there is no choice for the poet but to grit his teeth and comply. Perhaps poetry, in this case, is the only means of escape.

Time, once again, is a prominent theme in *Last Poems* 34, "The First of May." Housman juxtaposes two different conceptions of time: the cyclical, seasonal time of the natural world, and the linear time of the human lifespan. These figurations of time have additional and important associations: the natural cycles of the seasons correspond to traditional community life, as well as the "pagan" or non-Christian calendar. Traditional Mayday celebrations (such as the fair in this poem) originate in such customs. The human lifespan, being a linear and finite measure of time, corresponds closely to Christian eschatology. The scientific theories and industrial development of nineteenth Britain threatened the stability of both systems.

However, this poem does not privilege one kind of time over another. Seasonal time is springtime in *Last Poems* 34: but it is an endlessly repeated, static season. The images of growth and renewal—blooming orchards—are repeated in the first three stanzas. No tree "bears fruit," just as, by the conclusion, nothing is gained in terms of the speaker's youthful desires. Rather, having grown older and wiser, he has developed a jaded perspective: as he sees new generations of young men taking the place of his own, he can only reflect ironically that

> Our thoughts, a long while after,
> They think, our words they say;
> Theirs now's the laughter,
> The fair, the first of May.

Yet, there is a tone of nostalgia in this poem, especially in the second stanza, which is full of descriptive imagery and is relatively free of irony, save for the last line. The positive, and rather wistful, self-description could convey his wish to return to a state of innocent, youthful ignorance. His advanced perspective, however, supercedes this veiled wish. For now he is all too aware that the blossoming hopes of youth are never fulfilled—this is the "bitter fruit" of recognition that comes with age and frustrated experience. Living out one's allotted time on earth requires a resignation to the "sumless tale of sorrow" that is "all unrolled in vain."

There is another interesting and related juxtaposition in *Last Poems* 34, between the living and the dead. The bounty of spring in the natural world is only a kind of charade. This static spring is not productive; time stands still, as it does for the dead. The ancient Ludlow tower, symbol of history and community, is literally "*planted* on the dead*." But again, this is not fertile ground. The young men on their way to the fair will one day join those buried in the churchyard. These "sons of men," past and present, will not have achieved their own desires, let alone a greater understanding of human nature. The past is simply repeated in a timeless fashion, and neither these young men nor an entire culture appear to change in the process. Ironically, the speaker's world-weary perspective, always returning to invade the end of each stanza, cannot yield any lasting truths. His experience will die with him. In the speaker's eyes, it seems that the human nature of desire will invariably hinder or overpower any progress toward self-knowledge.

The interplay of human desire and man's relationship to nature is explored in *Last Poems* 40 "Tell me not here, it needs not saying." The poem's descriptive passages linger over details and create a painterly vision of the natural world:

> On acres of seeded grasses
> > The changing burnish heaves;
> Or marshalled under moons of harvest
> > Stand still at night the sheaves;
> Or beeches strip in storms for winter
> > And stain the wind with leaves.

This lush, abundant nature is one that also includes man: the poet must be involved with the landscape to provide such details, and the "sheaves" in particular are evidence of man's cultivation of the earth. This type of relationship initially suggests the poem's connection to nineteenth century Romanticism. In particular, the final lines of this stanza recall Shelley's "Ode to the West Wind."

However, this romantic, nostalgic tone also masks another type of relationship figured in the poem: the poets uses nature as a surrogate object of desire. In particular, this poem plays with the literary trope of the female body as a natural landscape—a landscape to be explored, lingered over, and possessed. In the poem, this body's unresponsiveness provokes the speaker's familiar resignation to disappointment, which is suggested in the past tense and moody tone of the first stanza:

> Tell me not here, it needs not saying,
>> What tune the enchantress plays ...
> For she and I were long acquainted
>> And I knew all her ways.

The poem also focuses on autumn, a time of dying away, and also of nature's "beguiling" swan-song. Lines such as "On russet floors, by waters idle," "The changing burnish heaves," "elmy plains and highways," "stain the wind with leaves" bring out the beauty of the season, and reveal the speaker's attachment to it. This time of dying is also one which allows the speaker to forget his own loss; he can fully immerse himself in the natural processes of decline around him, which—sensually—may still satisfy. Yet, just as autumn turns to winter, this too is a finite relationship.

It is important to note that this poem is an apostrophe, perhaps the reader; the speaker calls out to and literally resigns "these countries" to another. However, this seemingly passive act of resignation is also a type of confrontation. The reader is called upon, even challenged, to try to possess what the speaker seems or wishes to have possessed himself. Since the speaker already has experienced this possession as futile—or at the least, unrequited and anonymous, this makes an ironic statement about this desire to possess. Presumably, the speaker would desire the recognition of, or for, what he possesses, be it another person or some particular apprehension of the natural world. Yet he tells us in the final stanza that his feet might as well be another's treading the "dews of morning."

The dichotomy of desire—possession and regret—is played by other means as well in this last stanza. For instance, the word "trespass" in the final stanza suggests encroachment upon a limit, invasion, and even taboo. If we think of nature as a metaphor for a lover's body in this poem, these associations are quite relevant. In addition, "the dews of morning" may also be "the dews of mourning"—in this case, the speaker's mourning of what he cannot express or truly possess.

It is not surprising then, the poem's growing tone of disappointment or "mourning" culminates in the final stanza. The first two lines of the make a complex statement.

> For nature, heartless, witless nature,
> Will neither care nor know

The speaker, provoked by frustration, calls nature "heartless" and "witless,"—revealing a rather hostile attitude toward this "enchantress." Yet, as the Darwinian science of Housman's day demonstrated, the natural world *is* both heartless and witless; it is an intricate system of relationships, but relationships that can "neither care nor know." The human possession of, and emotional connection to nature will always be an unrequited desire under these circumstances. In the poem, the speaker concedes to this fact by the implication of anonymity in the final line.

# *Last Poems* 12, 34, and 40

## CLEANTH BROOKS ON HOUSMAN'S ROMANTICISM

[In this excerpt, Cleanth Brooks discusses Housman's relationship to earlier modes and traditions of Romanticism in English literature.]

A little while ago, I called Housman a romantic poet, a late romantic. If I have emphasized Housman the ironist, it is because I think his irony is important and that its presence does not make him the less a romanticist. But a more obvious aspect of his romanticism may be his treatment of nature.

Many of the poems—and not only those of *A Shropshire Lad*—are given a pastoral setting. The English countryside is everywhere in Housman's poetry. A typical appearance is revealed in the charming lyric which is printed on the back of your programs.[1] To see the cherry in blossom is one of the delights of the year, and how few years there are vouchsafed us in which to see it. Time is the enemy of delight and yet the cherry tree is the product of time. The very description of the springtime beauty is ominous: if "hung with snow" is a way of stressing the unbelievable whiteness of the blossoms, the phrase also hints of winter and the death to come.

But Housman's view of nature looks forward to our time rather than back to that of Wordsworth. If nature is lovely and offers man delight, she does not offer him solace or sustain him as Wordsworth was solaced and sustained. For between Wordsworth and Housman there interpose themselves Darwin and Huxley and Tindall—the whole achievement of Victorian science. The effect of this impact of science is not, of course, to make Housman love nature less: one could argue that it has rendered nature for him more poignantly beautiful. But his attitude toward nature is not that of the early Romantics and we must take into account this altered attitude if we are to understand his poems. ( ... )

Our immensely increased knowledge of nature has not destroyed her charm. Even the so-called scientific neutralization of nature has not done that—not at least for many of our poets. But it has altered their attitudes toward her and it has tended to stress man's sense of his alienation from nature. (Of course, even this sense of alienation is not strictly "modern"—I find it, for example, in Keats' "Ode to a Nightingale.") But the fact of alienation tends to be determinative for the modern nature poet. ( ... )

Housman expressed his characteristic attitude toward nature in the beautiful poem numbered xl in *Last Poems*, his farewell to nature. The matter of the poem is the speaker's resignation of his mistress Nature to another. The resignation is forced; he does not willingly relinquish her. He has possessed her too completely to feel that she is less than a part of himself and his appetite for her is not cloyed. At this moment of conscious relinquishment, nature has never been more compellingly the enchantress.

> Tell me not here, it needs not saying,
>     What tune the enchantress plays
> In aftermaths of soft September
>     Or tinder blanching mays,
> For she and I were long acquainted
>     And I knew all her ways.

How thorough is his knowledge of her ways is quietly but convincingly made good in the second and third stanzas.

> On russet floors, by waters idle,
>     The pine lets fall its cone;
> The cuckoo shouts all day at nothing
>     In leafy dells alone;
> And traveller's joy beguiles in autumn
>     Hearts that have lost their own.

> On acres of the seeded grasses
>     The changing burnish heaves;
> Or marshalled under moons of harvest
>     Stand still all night the sheaves;
> Or beeches strip in storms for winter
>     And stain the wind with leaves.

These beautiful stanzas do more than create a series of scenes from nature. They insinuate the speaker's claim to his possession of nature through an intimate knowledge of her ways. Each of the vignettes suggests the secret life of nature revealed to a rapt and solitary observer: the tap of the falling pine cone, audible only because the scene is hushed and breathless; the shouts of the solitary cuckoo, who seems to be calling to no other bird and not even to a human listener but with cheerful idiocy shouting "at nothing"; the flower called "traveller's joy" in the autumn sunshine silently extending to the joyless wayfarer its grace of self, the namesake of joy.

The "changing burnish" on the "acres of the seeded grasses," I take to be the shimmer of light that one sees play upon a hayfield in late summer when the wind heaves and ripples the long grass stems to catch the light. You who have seen it will know that "burnish" is not too extravagant a term, for the grass sometimes shimmers as if it were metallic. The wind that heaves the grass is a fitful wind of late summer. That which strips the beech trees of their leaves is a late autumn gale. But the third scene portrayed in this stanza—

> Or marshalled under moons of harvest
> Stand still all night the sheaves—

is windless: that is the point, I take it, of the statement that under the harvest moon the sheaves "Stand still all night." The secret life of nature is thus depicted through all weathers and throughout the round of the seasons. All of it has been observed by the speaker, all of it has been made his own possession through knowledge and is held now in memory. But the various scenes of the changing year are but the magic spells woven by the one enchantress.

The fourth stanza stresses his claim to possession. The first line rings the changes upon the word "possess" and the very last word of the stanza, the emphatic closing rime word, is "mine." But the action of the stanza is a relinquishment of his claims. The speaker conjures the companion to whom he speaks the poem to

> Possess, as I possessed a season,
>   The countries I resign,
> Where over elmy plains the highway
>   Would mount the hills and shine,
> And full of shade the pillared forest
>   Would murmur and be mine.

His claim to possession is based upon a shared experience, a secret knowledge, the kind of bond that unites two lovers who feel that they belong to each other. But in this instance, the beloved is nature; and nature is not one to recognize any lover's claim to possession.

> For nature, heartless, witless nature—

Nature is not only the fickle mistress, she is the idiot mistress, having no more mind than heart.

> For nature, heartless, witless nature,
>   Will neither care nor know
> What stranger's feet may find the meadow
>   And trespass there and go,
> Nor ask amid the dews of morning
>   If they are mine or no.

Nature, for all her attractiveness to man, is supremely indifferent to him. This is the bedrock fact upon which the poem comes to rest, but if the fact constitutes a primal irony, it is accepted in this poem without rancor or any fierce bitterness. The very charm of nature is the way in which she can give herself freely to all of us who will strenuously try to claim her. And moreover, if nature, in this last stanza, is heartless and witless, she is still as freshly beautiful as the morning. Notice how concretely Housman says this in the closing lines. Nature spreads her dewy meadow as virginally fresh for the imprint of the feet of the trespasser as for those of the old lover who would like to believe that he alone possessed her.

The attitude toward nature here is not Wordsworth's confident trust that "Nature never did betray / The heart that loved her." Yet the poem may be said to illustrate the Wordsworthian formula

> How exquisitely the individual Mind ...
> ... to the external World
> Is fitted:—and how exquisitely, too— ...
> The external World is fitted to the Mind.

True, it is Housman's mind, not Wordsworth's, that is fitted to the landscape here described; but the exquisite fitting is there just the same—so much so that the nature that Housman depicts seems to answer at every point the sensitive and melancholy mind that perceives it, and in its turn implies in its aloof and beautifully closed order the loneliness and austerity of the mind of its observer.

NOTE

1. *A Shropshire Lad* ii, printed on the program for Mr. Brooks's lecture, March 26, 1959.

—Cleanth Brooks, "Alfred Edward Housman." *A.E. Housman: A Collection of Critical Essays*, Christopher Ricks, ed. (Englewood Cliffs, NJ: Prentice-Hall, 1968): pp. 78–83.

## CHRISTOPHER RICKS ON "THE NATURE OF HOUSMAN'S POETRY"

[Christopher Ricks is an influential and prolific literary critic, editor, and Warren Professor of the Humanities at Boston University. His many publications include works on Milton, Tennyson, Keats, and T.S. Eliot. He is also general editor of *The New Oxford Book of Victorian Verse* (1987) and *The Oxford Book of English Verse* (1999). This essay considers the latent and literal meanings in Housman's poetry.]

Housman wrote a good deal of nonsense verse; Laurence Housman included 12 examples in *A.E.H.*, and 3 more were separately reprinted. H. W. Garrod took the view that "the nonsense verse was well worth having—who had believed, else, that Housman had it in him either to be happy or to write nonsense?" But were Carroll and Lear happy? And much of Housman's serious verse uses a method— of indirections, disparities, and emotional cross—currents that is at its clearest in nonsense-verse. What is said is not what is meant, but something is certainly meant. (Often one cannot but think that a Freudian thing is meant.) When you met an old man "whose nerves had given way," you "attended to his wants": by putting his head into the ants' nest, tying his hands, and filling his mouth with hay:

> He could not squeal distinctly,
>   And his arms would not go round;
> Yet he did not leave off making
>   A discontented sound.

What more natural at this than mild irritation?

> And I said "When old men's nerves give way,
>   How hard they are to please!"

Such a poem is not an allegory, but how long is it since madness was treated in such a way? And how and why was Wilde punished? "Oh they're taking him to prison for the colour of his hair"—that poem is in a way the greatest of Housman's nonsense-verses, moving out into a larger lunacy. "The Crocodile, or Public Decency" shows us how children, made ashamed of nakedness, sacrifice themselves when the crocodile calls:

> "Come, awful infant, come and be
> Dressed, if in nothing else in me."

Such poems—and there are many more—are not lacking in personal feelings; their force comes from the fact that no man could have had a more rigid sense of Public Decency than had Housman, even though in one vital respect it oppressed his deepest feelings. ( ... )

[C]ontrarieties and disparities of feeling fascinated Housman. In many of his more strangely powerful poems, the force comes from what is submerged, "obscure and latent," so it is not surprising that he was fond of that particular kind of pun which creates its double meaning by invoking but excluding. When Milton described something in Paradise as "wanton," his meaning did not just forget about the fallen sense of the word; it invoked it but excluded it, so that Eve's hair was "wanton (not *wanton*)." As the man waited to be hanged in Housman's "Eight O'Clock," he "heard the steeple / Sprinkle the quarters on the morning town." "Morning (not mourning)": the town does not mourn.

> The diamond tears adorning
> Thy low mound on the lea,
> Those are the tears of morning,
> That weeps, but not for thee.
> [*Last Poems*, xxvii]

"Morning (not mourning)." George Herbert, in "The Sonne," had applauded the English language:

> How neatly doe we give one onely name
> To parents issue and the sunnes bright starre!

Housman, more lugubriously but no more absurdly, relished the conflict between morning and mourning. When the nettle dances on the grave, "It nods and curtseys and recovers." "Recovers," as a term in dancing; the dead man does not recover in this or any (unspoken) sense. "Curtseys," as part of the dance; but the curtsey is hardly a courtesy—indeed to dance on a grave is traditionally the extreme discourtesy.

Housman's sure feeling for a subterranean link comes out in the finest such unspoken pun, in the magnificent and solitary reflection:

> When the bells justle in the tower
>   The hollow night amid,
> Then on my tongue the taste is sour
>   Of all I ever did.
>           [*Additional Poems*, ix]

When Laurence Housman printed this, he gave the alternative reading "Then to my heart the thought is sour." Without "tongue" and "taste," almost nothing is left. And this is not just because an immediacy of detail is lost. The almost uncanny connection between the sound of bells and the sour taste depends on "tongue." Bells have tongues. Emily Dickinson, a poet greater than Housman but not utterly different in kind, begins a poem:

> It was not Death, for I stood up,
> And all the Dead, lie down—
> It was not Night, for all the Bells
> Put out their Tongues, for Noon.

Housman was not punning; he would have been perfectly happy if the obscure force of his stanza (which he never published, though it seems to me one of the finest things he ever wrote) had come home without any sense of the bizarre, almost surrealist, connection between the bells and the taste. "Surrealist" may go too far, but it is worth remembering that the first (unauthorised) printing of these lines (1930) bore the title: "A Fragment preserved by oral tradition and said to have been composed by A. E. Housman in a dream." And what is the sourest taste of all?

> Instead of sweets, his ample palate took
> Savour of poisonous brass and metal sick.
>           (Keats, *Hyperion*, I. 188–9) ( ... )

My final example is one of Housman's best poems. Yet it does apparently take up an attitude that is almost silly or absurd. In "Tell me not here, it needs not saying," William Empson noticed the way in which each penultimate line breaks into Alcaics, and then offered a superb insight into how the poem works:

> I think the poem is wonderfully beautiful. But a secret gimmick may well be needed in it to overcome our resistances, because the thought must be about the silliest or most self-centered that has ever been expressed about Nature. Housman is offended with the scenery, when he pays a visit to his native place, because it does not remember the great man; this is very rude of it. But he has described it as a lover, so in a way the poem is only consistent to become jealous at the end. Perhaps the sentiment has more truth than one might think ... many English painters really are in love with the scenery of England, and nothing else, so they had much better give up their theoretical tiff with Nature and get back to painting it. The last verse of the poem, driving home the moral, is no longer tenderly hesitant and therefore has given up the Alcaic metre.
>
> *(British Journal of Aesthetics, 1962)*

Housman's attitude, which would be little more than silly if concerned only with Nature, turns into a curious kind of jealousy if it deals too with love of a woman. Of course the poem is magnificent as natural description; Housman's eye and ear were never more alert. But this straightforward, respectable and explicit feeling is entwined with a remarkable erotic force. Not that the poem is "really" erotic and not about Nature; it is about both. Housman, with disconcerting literalness, really does write about his mistress Nature as if she were his mistress. Hence the peculiar force derived from casting the poem in the form of a monologue from an old and cast-off lover to the young man who has succeeded him. You need not tell *me* about her, "for she and I were long acquainted." So that the act of resigning (a resignation stated, but still showing "the continuance of [his] first affection") is fraught with an intensity hard to understand if we think only of Nature:

> Possess, as I possessed a season,
>   The countries I resign.

Housman is taking seriously two conventions that are usually trifled with: that Nature is like a mistress, and that loving a mistress is like loving Nature (the long vogue for poems which describe love-making in topographical terms). There is the contrast between the unhurried rhythm and the momentary flash of bitterness in "a season," and there is the complete aptness of "Possess," emphatically placed and repeated. The enchantress was not just distantly *heard* on the new-mown grass or under the trees.

> On acres of the seeded grasses
> The changing burnish heaves ...

Are we to remember how Tennyson brings together love and Nature in *Locksley Hall*?

> In the Spring a livelier iris changes on the burnish'd dove;
> In the Spring a young man's fancy lightly turns to thoughts
> of love.

And surely it is not Just of Nature as *like* a mistress that we think when we hear how

> full of shade the pillared forest
> Would murmur and be mine.

The poem is not a code, and we cannot go through it looking for point-by-point correspondences. What we have is the co-existence of powerful love for Nature with powerful erotic feelings. It is in the last stanza that the bitterness makes itself heard; the poet is still in love with something he knows is heartless and witless (no substitute for the love of people). Lurking behind this attack on the faithless promiscuity of Nature is the traditional image for a promiscuous woman as "the wide world's common place," or "the bay where all men ride." Bitterness' perversity, and self-reproach are all fused by lyrical grace into a poem unique in the language.

—Christopher Ricks, "The Nature of Housman's Poetry." *A.E. Housman: A Collection of Critical Essays*, Christopher Ricks, ed. (Englewood Cliffs, NJ: Prentice-Hall, Inc., 1968): pp. 117–119, 120–122.

# R.L. KOWALCZYK ON HOUSMAN'S "VICTORIAN MALAISE"

[This excerpt explores Housman's relationship to Victorian culture and the ways in which his poetry reflects what Kowalczyk terms the "malaise" of the period, a condition resulting from scientific discoveries and the waning of religious belief in the Victorian period.]

Housman's poetry bears witness to the sense of isolation which permeates the poetry of the nineteenth century. We immediately recall Tennyson's dark mood in the first movement of *In Memoriam* as his commitment to science finds nature unsympathetic to his grief, a world that is ravenous, "fed in tooth and claw." Elsewhere, but particularly in "Dover Beach," Matthew Arnold lays bare the bleak, nineteenth-century promise of science:

> ... for the world, which seems
> So various, so beautiful, so new,
> Hath really neither joy, nor love, nor light,
> Nor certitude, nor peace, nor help for pain;
> And we are here as on a darkling plain
> Swept with confused alarms of struggle and flight,
> Where ignorant armies clash by night. (pub. 1867)

Gerard Manley Hopkins' dark sonnets, likewise, evoke the terrifying experience of isolation when the loving face of God departed from his sight. Thomas Hardy's quarrel with the impersonal universe takes form in his concept of the Immanent Will, an unfeeling, vast, unperceiving force which created man and his world, and forgot to destroy them.

Housman's sense of disorientation in the immensity of the cosmos finds, first of all, no assurance in a benevolent Deity. In *ASL* XLVII, for example, Housman chooses the Golgotha scene of Christ's passion and places it in the Shropshire setting to express the driftless futility of life. Although the setting obscures the poet's irreverence, the poet denies Christ's power over the forces of evil and suggests man's inadequacy in the world. The carpenter's son hangs between two thieves, because he left his home and trade to change the condition of man. The speaker's tone is full of regret; he finds little consolation in his love for man: "All the same's the luck we prove, / Though the midmost hangs for love." Addressing his comrades, the condemned carpenter urges them to follow another path—"Live, lads, and I will die"—and he reminds them that if he had passively accepted the conditions of existence,

> Then I might have built perhaps
> Gallow-trees for other chaps,
> Never dangled on my own
> —Had I but left ill alone.

In the poem we hear the voice of suffering man, abandoned, overwhelmed by the enormities of existence. Unlike the Christian belief in the prevailing power of love, the speaker's blank regret denies the efficacy of benevolence in the world. Housman's view, then, may be interpreted as a discomforting explanation of Christianity in its death throes. ( ... )

In *Last Poems* XII, Housman identifies Providential workings and civil laws; in both he recognizes the powers of impersonalism:

> The laws of God, the laws of man,
> He may keep that will and can;
> Not I: let God and man decree
> Laws for themselves and not for me;
> And if my ways are not theirs
> Let them mind their own affairs.

Line three explodes in ambiguity; it is not yet clear whether the shocking "Not I," in line three, means that the poet refuses to submit to divine and civil laws, or whether he is unable to obey them. This ambiguity reflects a state of mind which sees the "new earth" as tyrannical, governed by capricious gods and capricious men:

> But no, they will not; they must still
> Wrest their neighbors to their will,
> And make me dance as they desire
> With jail and gallows and hell-fire.

Here, the image of man as a puppet contextually controls the poem's theme: traditional bromides (divine and civil powers protect man from evil) bewilder men and fail to protect them from the hostilities of existence. The poet confronts the problem of submitting to laws which are "foreign" to his nature. His alternative is to reject both sources of authority in cynical abandonment found similarly in Arnold's "Mycerinus" and in Fitzgerald's *Rubaiyat of Omar Khayyam*. The last six lines of the poem present Housman's choice. Since he cannot return to the ancient gods, Saturn and Mercury (the implication being that all the gods are dead) he will observe the Christian code for formality's sake, whether it be "right or wrong" or "foolish." ( ... )

Regarding man's relationship to nature, the new science leads Housman to one compelling conclusion:

> Tell me not here, it needs not saying,
>     What tune the enchantress plays
> In aftermaths of soft September
>     Or under blanching Mays,
> For she and I were long acquainted
>     And I knew all her ways....
>
> For Nature, heartless, witless nature,
>     Will neither care nor know
> What stranger's feet may find the meadow
>     And trespass there and go,
> Nor ask amid the dews of morning
>     If they are mine or no.

Man does not posses nor control nature; he is, rather, a possession himself, yoked to nature's changeless laws. Left without the consoling bond of divine Consciousness and of its loving direction, Housman views the world around him in its most frightening aspect. Like Arnold's Empedocles on Mount Etna, Housman's poetic characters fail to find divine love in the universe. They confront the enormity of space and realize that they are victims of Nature's blind forces. A number of Housman's lyrics scrutinize with cool, detached irony the impersonal universe, the vicious world in which man was placed to endure his fated existence. ( ... )

The sense of inevitability, to which Victorian doubt often led, verifies for Housman the continuous cycle of man's painful existence. *Last Poems* XXXVIII, for example, concentrates upon this nineteenth century malady. The poet gives equal treatment to three stages of the day, which he describes with imagery suggestive of night:

> Now dreary dawns the eastern light.
>     And fall of eve is drear,
> And cold the poor man lies at night,
>     And so goes out the year.

The allusion to the passage of time from sunrise to sunset, from year to year, signifies a continuum in the process of man's driftless life. In the next stanza, Housman reverts to a favorite device by interjecting a personal comment as a standard example of all men's experiences:

> Little is the luck I've had
>     And oh, 'tis comfort small
> To think that many another lad
>     Has had no luck at all.

This stanza damages the effect of the previous four lines, partly because it is repetitious and partly because Housman shifts the mood and point of view. Still, the flat statements in the stanza recognize a bleak fellowship which offers man little comfort. The tension in Housman's poetry, then, represents a voice born out of the time when scientific discoveries no longer allowed men to see the correlation between Nature and a spiritual world, as the Romantic William Wordsworth did in the earlier nineteenth century. The empirical, naturalistic scrutiny of Charles Darwin, Thomas Henry Huxley and Herbert Spencer revealed Nature to be the unfeeling phenomena of cyclical forces and laws. The implications derived from this viewpoint, about the dignity of human nature in an impersonal world, formulated for Housman a recurring theme, one with which he was to wrestle in vain. ( ... )

Thus, I have tried to suggest that Housman's poetic vision is a reaction to Victorian disquiet, to the belief that human events move in a limited, circular path, restricted in its motion by the cycles of change and time, leading nowhere except toward the oblivion of final extinction. The only acceptable view of life to Housman in his reluctant recognition of existence as the organic growth of evil. His position rejects the optimism of philosophy and the consolation of theology with a mathematically calculated certainty found in the science which destroyed his serenity and peace. He divorces himself from his Christian heritage and commits himself to a sober pejorism. This commitment clarifies Housman's fear and his concern for the demands of time. In *A Shropshire Lad* he transforms the pastoral setting (the dream world of the past) into its contemporary counterpart, Shropshire. The Shropshire rustics, with whom Housman associates all human experience, are impregnated with the sense of time and of the immensity of the world in which they live. Time and space condition their hollow attempts to give some meaning to their brief and discontented lives. Their actions—the drunkenness, the love-making, the enlistments, the violence—are frantic efforts of men to ward off the advancement of old age and deteriorations of youthful vitality. Upon birth they find themselves judged and condemned by time to one destiny, final extinction.

—R.L. Kowalczyk, "Victorian Malaise and the Poetry of A.E. Housman." *Cithara* 6:2, May 1967: pp. 13–14, 15–16, 19–20.

## KENNETH WOMACK ON HISTORICIZING HOUSMAN'S POETRY

[Kenneth Womack is Assistant Professor of English at Penn State, Altoona. He is the coeditor of *Twentieth-Century Bibliography and Textual Critcism: An Annotated Bibliography*, and has edited three volumes of the *Dictionary of Literary Biography*. His essay considers Housman's work in the historical and atheistic contexts of scientific tradition and Epicurean Philosophy.]

In his 1911 Cambridge Inaugural Lecture, A. E. Housman alluded to the same scientific and natural laws that informed, thematically and ideologically, much of his earlier poetic *oeuvre*: 'This fright, this night of the mind, must be dispelled not by the rays of the sun, nor day's bright spears, but by the face of nature and her laws. And this is her first, from which we take our start: nothing was ever by miracle made from nothing' (26). In this remarkably Lucretian phrase, as well as in his own work as poet and classical editor, Housman reveals his great regard for Lucretius and his ancient philosophy. Housman's admiration for Lucretius has indeed been well-documented; he once praised the poet-philosopher's *De Rerum Natura* lovingly as 'a work more compact of excellence than any edition of any classic produced in England' (Graves, 1979, p. 166). Lucretius' Epicurean ontology profoundly influenced Housman's poetry, particularly in the poet's 1896 volume, *A Shropshire Lad*, while at the same time impinging upon Housman's own interest in the means of human existence and the *topos* of atomic theory— Lucretian concepts that fathered the notion of 'the stuff of life' so prevalent in Housman's poetry.[1]

A reading of Housman's work in regard to the scientific naturalism of Victorian England, particularly through the essays of Thomas Henry Huxley, reveals a post-Victorian aesthetic informed by the scientific pursuits and conclusions of another era—not only from the age of Lucretius, as previous critics have astutely noted, but from the age of Darwin as well. In this manner, then, Victorian science informs the historical dynamic of Housman's poetics and thus merges with his latent Lucretian ideology to produce a complex historical amalgam comprising competing scientific philosophies from dramatically divergent historical moments. At the same time, such a conclusion underscores the value of Jerome J. McGann's programme for historical-literary study, originally promulgated in his 1985 volume, *The Beauty of Inflections: Literary Investigations in Historical Method and Theory*. McGann writes: 'Poems at once locate a dialectical encounter between the past and the present, and they represent, through processes of reflection, a particular instance of dialectical exchange which is taken in the present as given and through the past' (p. 5). Considering Housman's poetry as a venue for the historical interplay between ancient and Victorian scientific beliefs—particularly in regard to McGann's relevant post-structuralist concerns for matters of historicity—enables critics to revise their ideas concerning the manner in which Housman forged his aesthetic, while at the same time allowing them to unearth further the Victorian ideals embedded in Housman's remarkable verse.[2]

To understand fully Housman's appropriation of ancient philosophy in his poetics, the respective philosophies of Epicurus and Lucretius must first be elucidated. ( ... )

Epicurean philosophy *per se* functions upon three basic principles. First, Epicurus argues that all pleasure is good, while all evil is bad. The second basic tenet of Epicurean philosophy arises directly from the concepts of good and evil. Epicurus believed that death was a natural part of humanity—an experience not to be feared, but to be embraced (Rosenbaum, 1986, pp. 217–18). In *On Nature*, Epicurus argues that to the living, death remains an unknown quantity, thus producing an understandable human fear. Epicurus believed that such a fear was ludicrous because man has no basis for understanding the experience of death, only the expectation of it: 'Foolish, therefore, is the man who says that he fears death, not because it will pain when it comes, but because it pains in the prospect' (Rosenbaum, 1989, p. 82). As Epicurus argues, the fear of death is grounded merely in its expectation; without any knowledge about the experience of death, man can only wait and ponder the possibility of no longer existing.

The final principal tenet of Epicurean philosophy relates to the existence of atoms. Epicurus drew his conclusions regarding atoms from another ancient philosopher. ( ... )

Epicurus believed that atoms were both indivisible and indestructible, and thus they could not be created by man. Accordingly, Epicurus believed that the body in its living state is made up of a finite number of atoms that comprise the human soul. According to the Epicurean ontology, when the body enters a state of death, its atoms are immediately dispersed into the world, thus becoming free to form another being. In this manner, Epicurus offers an important observation about the mortality of the human soul and suggests that through death, the body and the soul enter into a permanent state of non-existence (Copley, pp. xi–xiii). Further, this observation remains one of the primary philosophical underpinnings of Housman's early poetry.

One of Epicurus' earliest disciples was the ancient poet, Lucretius, who is believed to have lived between 95 and 52 BC (Copley, p. viii). Lucretius embraced Epicureanism, especially Epicurus' three principal tenets and his forays into atomic theory (Copley, pp. xvi–xvii). Lucretius prominently features these Epicurean ideals in *De Rerum Natura*, particularly in Book Three of his long poem. In this instance, Lucretius explores the Epicurean belief that death remains an unknown experience—again, an experience not to be feared but embraced. Lucretius wrote: 'Often through fear of death men come to hate life and the sight of the sun so bitterly that in a burst of grief they kill themselves, forgetting that it was this fear that caused their cares, troubled their conscience, broke their bonds of friendship, and overturned all sense of decency' (pp. 58–9). Thus, in Lucretius' philosophical purview, the fear of death breeds a fear of living. ( ... )

Life, according to the Epicurean argument, creates the restraint that holds the atoms within the body. In death, however, the atoms are released to pursue their own free will. As Lucretius writes: 'Say it again: when all our fleshy husk is loosened, and the breath of life cast out, you must admit that sensate soul and mind break up; a single life links soul and body' (p. 70). In this way, then, Lucretius suggests that with the exodus of atoms, the body and the soul cease to exist. ( ... )

Two thousand years later, a series of essays by Thomas Henry Huxley revealed the scientist's latent Epicurean ideals in his Victorian-era criticisms of the work of British naturalist, Charles Darwin—critical studies that offer a relevant discourse on several issues of an Epicurean nature. For example, in his 1868 essay, 'On the Physical Basis of Life', Huxley considers the same questions that Epicurus surely must have pondered years before:

And now, what is the ultimate fate, and what the origin, of the matter of life? Is it, as some of the older naturalists supposed, diffused throughout the universe in molecules, which are indestructible and, unchangeable in themselves; but, in endless transmigration, unite in innumerable permutations, into the diversified forms of life we know? Or, is the matter of life composed of ordinary matter, and again resolved into ordinary matter when its work is done?

(p. 145) ( ... )

In his poetry, Housman, in the tradition of Lucretius and Huxley, operated from an ontology in his work that remains strikingly Epicurean. Housman's poetry and prose contain several examples of Epicurean concepts, particularly in relation to atomic theory, mortality and the human fear of death. As his brother Laurence recalled, in religious matters Housman approved of the Church of England as an institution, yet possessed no faith in its tenets (Haber, 1967, p. 164). Critics such as Richard Perceval Graves ascribe Housman's affinity for the philosophies of Epicurus and Lucretius— and later, Huxley—to their atheism. As Graves notes, Lucretius' 'main work [De Rerum Natura] was a savage attack upon religious belief' (p. 203). Housman, both a contemporary of Huxley[3] and also agnostic in his beliefs, believed that the soul was as mortal as the body and had strong reservations about the notion of immortality.

As Norman Marlow argues, 'One can sense in Housman, as in Huxley, Romanes, and other agnostics of the late nineteenth century, the underlying bewilderment and anguish of a soul naturally Christian, ... yet to call Housman a Christian, as some have done, is of course nonsense' (p. 152). ( ... )

Like Lucretius, Housman believed that the human fear of death precluded any real and productive means of existence, and an examination of his poetry reveals the manner in which he employs—again, like Lucretius—the tenets of atomic theory in an effort to demonstrate the vacuous nature of human life in the enduring face of death.

The poet also entertained similar notions regarding Epicurean atomic theory, arguments previously considered by Lucretius and Huxley. In Poem XXXI from *A Shropshire Lad*, Housman offers images of the gale of life as it blows through the fictive terrain of the poet's Shropshire, spreading the ashes and atoms of the narrator's human precursors among the shadows of his fleeting contemporary existence:

> There, like the wind through woods in riot,
>   Through him the gale of life blew high;
> The tree of man was never quiet:
>   Then 'twas the Roman, now 'tis I.
>
> The gale, it plies the saplings double,
>   It blows so hard, 'twill soon be gone:
> To-day the Roman and his trouble
>   Are ashes under Uricon.

Norman Page argues that the movements of the wind in *A Shropshire Lad* function as a poetic manoeuvre that enables Housman to forge a temporal link between the ancient past, a dismal present and an uncertain future: 'The wind blows not just through a human life but through history,' Page writes; 'the wind of the distant past ... links dead Roman and Victorian Englishman' (1983, p. 195). In this way, Housman alludes—through his references to the enduring winds of ancient Uricon—to the phenomenon that Tom Burns Haber calls the 'unending cycle of atomic dissolution and recombination' prevalent throughout the poet's verse (1967, p. 164).

Housman offers similar images of the wind as a means of posthumous transport in Poem XXXII from *A Shropshire Lad*, a poem where Housman continues to posit his overarching argument regarding atomic theory. The manner in which Housman employs his Epicurean thesis across the boundaries of his various poetic entries in *A Shropshire Lad* underscores the poet's insistence upon the value of atomic theory and its ancient philosophical properties, while also affirming Page's assertion that 'almost any individual poem in *A Shropshire Lad* has a total meaning that is partly supplied by its relationship to other poems in the collection. This relationship may be thematic or it may be a matter of recurrent diction or imagery' (1983, p. 195). In the following instance from Poem XXXII, the poem's narrator again discusses the existence of atoms—the 'stuff of life'—and the way in which they combined to form his very being:

> From far, from eve and morning
> And yon twelve-winded sky,
> The stuff of life to knit me
> Blew hither: here am I.

In the second stanza, the narrator warns that he has not yet 'dispersed', referring to his own inevitable death and atomic dissolution, as well as to the larger, Epicurean ontological construct of atomic dispersal. Through this ancient metaphor, the narrator acknowledges the fleeting nature of his existence:

> Now—for a breath I tarry
> Nor yet disperse apart—
> Take my hand quick and tell me,
> What have you in your heart.

The images of fortuitously swerving atoms in these lines are vivid indeed, and, as Haber notes, Poem XXXII 'can be understood only in terms of Lucretius' atomistic theory' (1967, p. 162). John Bayley also argues that this instance in Poem XXXII offers additional images of 'urgency ... heightened into mysteriousness'—emotions no doubt intensified by Housman's arguments, via Lucretius, regarding the tenuous nature of human life. As Bayley concludes: 'A lifetime should be enough for any number of such exchanges, but the poem sees the whole of it as a moment' (1992, p. 34).

Yet another poem from *A Shropshire Lad*, Poem XLIII ('The Immortal Part'), echoes Lucretian and Epicurean ideals as well. In this poem, the narrator suggests that the only immortal part of the body is the bone, rather than the soul—the conclusion of the more popular religious beliefs of Housman's era. As Marlow remarks, 'Housman himself never speaks of his atheism more directly' than in 'The Immortal Part' (1958, p. 53). When the narrator refers to a voice within him, he refers not to his immortal Christian soul, but instead to his aching bones, appendages exhausted from the chores of living:

> When I meet the morning beam
> Or lay me down at night to dream,
> I hear my bones within me say,
> 'Another night, another day'.

In this instance—and within Housman's larger aesthetic—the bones trudge on, for they are the true immortal parts, and long after the narrator's life has ceased, his bones will continue to endure:

> Before this fire of sense decay,
> This smoke of thought blow clean away,
> And leave with ancient night alone
> The stedfast and enduring bone.

As Cleanth Brooks notes, 'The Immortal Part' offers a paradox because 'the immortal part of man is his skeleton—not the spirit, not the soul—but the most earthy, the most nearly mineral part of his body' (1968, p. 70). Such a conclusion is reminiscent of Huxley's own scepticism about the soul as a living feature within the human body. For this reason, Housman conspicuously avoids any explanation for the location of the soul, while instead providing his readers with the lasting image of a 'stedfast and enduring bone'— humanity's true immortal part, destined to live for centuries.

NOTES

1. The author would like to thank William Baker, Roy Birch, Charmian Hearne, Terence A. Hoagwood and Alan Holden for their encouragement and advice throughout the production of this essay.

2. Notably, Housman's verse—often lauded by his critics for its simplicity of form and meaning—in fact offers little in the way of poetic resolution. As John Peale Bishop remarks: 'Despite an apparent clarity such that almost any poem seems ready to deliver its meaning at once, there is always something that is not clear, something not brought into the open, something that is left in doubt' (1940, p. 141). As this essay will demonstrate, the complexity of the philosophy

endemic to Housman's opaque aesthetic finds its roots in the very confusion and doubt of which Bishop speaks, and the poet deliberately appropriates such a hazy tableau in order to posit his arguments regarding atomic theory and the fleeting nature of human life.

3. In a letter to Max Beerbohm of 16 May 1933, Housman refers in poetic jest to his Victorian contemporary. 'I also have a vision of grandpapa and great-grandpapa reading the works of Mr. Aldous Huxley, with the legend,' he writes: 'T. H. Huxley Esq., P.C. / Is this how Leonard bred his brat? / The Rev. T. Arnold, D.D. / Good Gracious! even worse than Matt' (*Letters*, 1971, p. 334).

—Kenneth Womack, "'Ashes Under Uricon': Historicizing A.E. Housman, Reifying T.H. Huxley, Embracing Lucretius." *A.E. Housman: A Reassessment*, Alan W. Holden and J. Roy Birch, eds. (New York: MacMillan and St. Martin's Press, 2000). 76–86.

# HOUSMAN'S MYTHIC FIGURATIONS

## CRITICAL ANALYSIS OF

# *A Shropshire Lad* 22 and 47

The prominent military motif in Housman's poems participates significantly with his poetry's active mythologizing. At the least, *A Shropshire Lad* and the later books make no secret of Terence Hearsay's (or the poet's) admiration of soldiers and the imagined, idealized world they have come to represent for him, as well as a concurrent frustration with his own life. Two key aspects of the Shropshire mythology are sexuality and death, and the very nature of these subjects propels them into conflict with the poet's implied attitude toward God, religious belief, and human nature.

One military poem that demonstrates this mythologizing process, and in particular how a mythology is constructed around secret desire, is *A Shropshire Lad* 22 "The street sounds to the soldiers' tread." The poem describes the poet's simple encounter—or rather, mere eye contact—with a soldier in the street, as the troops are marching off to war. The remarkable nature of this poem is what it does with such an apparent 'non-event.' This encounter expands geographically, psychologically, and emotionally, to establish a larger—albeit subtle—narrative about unacknowledged desire, unfulfilled possibilities, the potential for kinship, and the speaker's alienation. This meta-narrative lends the poem its poignancy and supports its allusions to loss, love, and regret; in this sense it also contributes significantly to the entire Shropshire mythology.

The first stanza of *Shropshire* 22 establishes a context of "equalization;" although the townspeople ostensibly admire and esteem the soldiers, they "troop out," like soldiers themselves, to see them. This verb puts the two groups on "equal footing," as it were. More importantly, it creates a world in which soldier and townsman can have a mutual experience of personal connection, by way of mere eye contact. The plain description of this encounter belies its emotional implications; the redundancy in "he turns" is a key to the excitement and intensity of feeling this simple movement creates in the speaker.

> A single redcoat turns his head
> He turns to look at me.

In the second stanza, this interpersonal bond set up by the "look" is expanded geographically, from the Shropshire sky to "sky's so far." Moreover, the "he" and "I" of the first stanza is now a "we." Although the speaker knows he will be "leagues apart" from this man and may never see him again, they are now inextricably bound together, by his imagination and by language. This meeting of townsman and soldier, which is both the first and the last meeting, is at once a realistic description of encounter, and a comment on the fugitive nature of the speaker's desire—the fleeting prospect of homosexual love. The emotional component of the poem is elaborated in the final stanza, as the speaker now comments on himself and the soldier as a kind of couple. Neither can "stop to tell" what thoughts and feelings may be rushing through them, but the speaker essentially projects himself into the soldier's mind and heart by assuming there is anything at all *to* tell. These two lines also comment on the toll that war takes on human relationships; whatever each man may be feeling is rendered meaningless and irrelevant in the nation's march to war.

Ironically, this stanza also highlights the denial of desire that is also at work in the poem. The impossibility of extending the action beyond a single glance, the impossibility of "stopping to tell" has been preceded by other of negatives to create a series of "no's": "We never crossed before," "We're like to meet no more." Moreover, we read in the last lines a kind of emotional retreat. Although all the speaker can really do is wish the soldier well, this individual has now become an "everyman." "[D]ead or living, drunk or dry" describes the conditions of any number of soldiers; it also generalizes this particular soldier's fate, thrusting him back into the nameless body of troops marching through town. Through this reversal, the poet's desire is also denied, and made so general as to escape notice. The final two lines' implied distance of time and space renders the speaker's erotic connection to the soldier into a kind, unconditional, and anonymous compassion.

Mythmaking takes a different turn in *A Shropshire Lad* 47, "The Carpenter's Son," which is a re-imagining of the crucifixion. The speaker is now a Christ-figure, and begins the poem, appropriately, by distancing himself from onlookers and friends—"lads." However, his difference is not of a spiritual nature, rather he bears the mark of Cain; he has committed a crime of some kind, some grave mistake. "Had I stuck to plane and adze / I had not been lost, my lads." Not only does the poet re-imagine the crucifixion in a wholly secular, and rather pedestrian, context but he is merely a "carpenter's son." And this man's experience, for which he now hangs, is also secularized. Instead of revelation or miracle, the poem repeatedly presents us with a situation entirely 'of this world' and very human—a mistake or crime has been committed, some kind of "ill." This word appears throughout the poem—either as the speaker's self-characterization, "ill fare I"; a description of the unnamed crime, "had I but left ill alone," or an assessment of where he now stands: "So 'tis come from ill to worse." Repetition of the word accentuates the poem's conceit that the speaker is himself "ill," "not right," and ultimately, criminal.

Crucifixions were not merely cruel punishments, their public nature served as a warning, an assertion of a ruler's or community's common power over the individual. The speaker comments on this, as well as his own community role. If his secret "ill" had not been found out, he'd be no different from those other lads, his peers; he would still be a part of their community, upholding its moral and legal code by building "Gallow's-trees for other chaps."

The speaker's mysterious crime and Jesus's crucifixion are ironically superimposed in the fifth stanza, and it is through this irony we are given a hint as to the nature of his crime, or "ill." Just as Jesus hung between two thieves, so does the speaker; just as Jesus "died for love," so does our speaker. However, because the poem has thus far described an entirely secular context, we know that the speaker's love is not the same as Jesus's. If Jesus, the "son of man," died for God's love of man, then the speaker is dying for one thing only: man's love of man.

The final stanzas reiterate the crime, without naming it, and the address to other men in the opening stanza takes on another level of meaning. "Comrades all" implies a kinship with the poet, and by extension, some understanding of his dilemma. The speaker warns them against the same mistake—that is, dying or sacrificing one's own life for a man's love—and implores them be shrewd, in other words, to understand the rules of the world they live in, and act accordingly. His dying injunction to "walk henceforth in other ways," is thus an act of persuasion: to live, they must choose another sort of "decent" love.

CRITICAL VIEWS ON

# *A Shropshire Lad* 22 and 47

## CHARLES WILLIAMS ON HOUSMAN'S RESIGNATION AND THE SUBLIMATION OF DEATH

[Charles Williams was an English poet, novelist, critic, reviewer, and biographer, working primarily at Oxford University Press. His published works include cycles of Arthurian poetry, as well as *Poetry at Present*, in which this essay appeared. In this excerpt, Williams provides a general overview of the themes and rhetorical effects at work in Housman's poems and the way these structure the poet's mythical Shropshire.]

No living poet has presented work of such small extent, such unvarying perfection, such renewed intensity, and such catastrophic despair. The illusion, the dream, the desire that things ought to be different, have here no place. Mr. Housman has invented no god to blame; he has, it seems, left behind, so far as man can, even the wish for happiness. Perfect in word, perfect in spirit, these poems arise from a depth of bitter resignation which has not hitherto found expression in English verse. There have been cries of romantic personal despair, but this verse is classic in its restraint and calm balance.

Not that every poem is explicitly concerned with the 'much less good than ill'. A reader who opened *A Shropshire Lad* at the beginning could read the first sixteen poems without finding in it more than an occasional stanza of darkness, and without necessarily holding it to be more than dramatic or semi-dramatic. For those sixteen contain love-songs, a ballad lyric, and one or two as exquisite nature-poems as any in English, especially the famous 'Loveliest of trees, the cherry now' which ends

> And since to look at things in bloom
> Fifty springs are little room,
> About the woodlands I will go
> To see the cherry hung with snow.

This satisfying stanza might have been written by a young romantic poet; the sense of death is used as it is used in Nash's 'Queens have died young and fair'; it seems to be allied to Romeo's great outcry and Keats's 'cease upon the midnight with no pain'. It is only in the seventeenth poem that there certainly enters another style of verse, where the young cricketer mocks at his own occupation—

> See the son of grief at cricket
> Trying to be glad.
>
> Try I will; no harm in trying.
> Wonder 'tis how little mirth
> Keeps the bones of man from lying
> on the bed of earth.

Grief is here no longer a delicious mood accentuating the contemplation of beauty, but the natural state of man from which he is tempted to escape by death. And as the reader passes on he finds that this state is the one in which Mr. Housman's imagination normally perceives man to be, but that grief is too small a name for it. It has no cause, for any momentary cause to which it might be attributed is less than itself.

> The troubles of our proud and angry dust
> Arc from eternity and shall not fail.

Here are poems enough on broken or thwarted love, of man for woman or of man for man; enough on parting, and the life and death of soldiers; enough on those who in the past or present are put to death by their fellows. To explain all these things Mr. Hardy has recourse to a metaphysic, but Mr. Housman will have nothing to do with any such attempt to ease the intellect. Mr. Hardy has invented or borrowed a god to argue with; Mr. Housman dismisses the First Cause in a line—'whatever brute or blackguard made the world'. Some laws, it seems, that First Cause has made; some laws, certainly, man. And these laws, if we can, we had better keep.

> How am I to face the odds
> Of man's bedevilment and God's?
> I, a stranger and afraid
> In the world I never made. [sic]

The motive is not really cowardice; it is rather that since we can do no better we had better do that.

It is inevitable that, with such a theme, and with certain poems which are a direct encouragement to suicide, the question of suicide should be raised. The business of a poet, of course, anyhow of a poet of a certain kind, is to express his imagination of the universe. Whether that imagination has any practical effect on our lives, and if so what, is a question for us and not for him, and it is an impertinence for us to inquire what effect it has had on his own. Nor is it to be overlooked that by the varying subjects and varying moods of and in which these poems are written, Mr. Housman has created almost everywhere a semi-dramatic effect. But if a poet has given us an harmonious imagination of life it is all the more satisfactory if a mere intellectual question arising out of it can be shown to be answered by its very nature. If we ask these two small books, 'But why should a man go on living?' an answer is there; there are several answers. The first is that, though life is an enemy, death is also an enemy. The exquisite sense of beauty, expressed in the highest form of traditional poetry, is too dear to be parted with—'the cherry hung with snow,' 'the silver sail of dawn',

> The Sun at noon to higher air
> Unharnessing the silver Pair
> That late before his chariot swam,

and so on.

> Could man be drunk for ever
>   With liquor, love, and fights—

but he can be drunk so long with such love that only in the very last crisis will he give up the indulgence, though he pays for it in his sober moments. Secondly, if those sober moments are too agonizing he will, anyhow, end them. It is the old undeniable answer—nothing is intolerable, for when indeed things are intolerable we die, either by our own will or against it.

The third and fourth answers are so much in the very heart of this verse that it is ridiculous to speak of them as 'answers' at all. They go before the question; they prevent it being asked; they are part of the nature of things which the verse is marvellously expressing. But in so far as they can be spoken of separately, the third answer is that we go on because we have to go on. Call it self-preservation, call it duty, call it what you will when a name for it is demanded, part of man's very burden is that he is so intensely alive that he is reluctant to cease. 'The troubles of our proud and angry dust' are not quite intolerable; 'bear them we can, and if we can we must'. We cannot die until we can, and when we can we do. Man has become conscious of his nature, and this is his nature. He lives, not from self-preservation or from moral duty, but from something more profound which he only knows because it is himself.

The last answer, put crudely and impossibly, is friendship. Friendship has not been praised so highly as it should have been; of this dearest mitigation of human existence the great poets seem to have been careless in their verse. Perhaps the long preoccupation with romantic and sexual love has caused its serener satisfaction to be neglected, even when it accompanies and is part of that other love. But Mr. Housman, who has no concern for romantic love except as a keen and often thwarted delight, has restored the love between friends to something approaching its right place. When the two books have been read this is left in the mind as the chief satisfaction, the most enduring peace of man. That many of the poems are on exile from friends—either by death or absence—makes no difference. The first poem in the *Shropshire Lad* is on the companionship of men of the same regiment; the last poem in *Last Poems* is on the communal dance at evening on the village green 'at Abdon under Clu' [*sic*]. Between them many of the 104 poems look to the love between friends as their subject or speak of it in their phrases. But perhaps that of all which prints it most clearly on the reader's mind is the poem called *Hell-Gate*. There the poet, with the devil by his side, approaches the gate of hell, where sit Death and Sin, and 'the damned in turn Pace for sentinel and burn'. When they come near

> the sentry turned his head,
> Looked, and knew me, and was Ned.

Recognizing his friend, the sentinel straddles across the way lest he should enter.

> But across the entry barred
> Straddled the revolted guard,
> Weaponed and accoutred well
> From the arsenals of hell;
> And beside him, sick and white,

Sin to left and Death to right
Turned a countenance of fear
On the flaming mutineer.
Over us the darkness bowed,
And the anger in the cloud
Clenched the lightning for the stroke;
But the traitor musket spoke.

And the hollowness of hell
Sounded as its master fell,
And the mourning echo rolled
Ruin through his kingdom old.
Tyranny and terror flown
Left a pair of friends alone,
And beneath the nether sky
All that stirred was he and I.

Silent, nothing found to say,
We began the backward way;
And the ebbing lustre died
From the soldier at my side,
As in all his spruce attire
Failed the everlasting fire.
Midmost of the homeward track
Once we listened and looked back;
But the city, dusk and mute,
Slept, and there was no pursuit.

It is the strangest and one of the finest of Mr. Housman's poems: strange because in some ways it is so unlike him—with its old mythology and its entire peace, and in some ways so like him, with its colloquial and convincing phrases. Many things have been said at hell gate since Dante and Milton passed there, but few phrases are so satisfying as that of this newcomer; to Sin's smile

'Met again, my lass', said I.

It is as great in its way as Farinata in his burning tomb.

—Charles Williams, "A.E. Housman," in *Poetry at Present* (Oxford: Calrendon Press, 1930). Reprinted in *A.E. Housman: The Critical Heritage*, Philip Gardner, ed. (London and New York: Routledge, 1992): pp. 226–231.

# STEPHEN SPENDER ON THE "ESSENTIAL HOUSMAN"

[Stephen Spender was a distinguished poet, critic, lecturer, and editor. His works include *The Still Centre*, *Poems of Dedication*, and *The Generous Days*. Spender was a Professor of English at University College, London, and was knighted in 1983. This excerpt contextualizes Housman's poetics within the traditions of English and European poetry, and suggests how Housman's method and poetic preoccupations help to create particular and consistent mythologies in and about his work.]

At his best, Housman is a poet of great force and passion whose music is quite unforced, combining sensuousness with a cold discipline which gives the poetry an almost anonymous quality of being something said rightly, rather than something said by someone:

> A Grecian lad, as I hear tell,
>   One that many loved in vain,
> Looked into a forest well
>   And never looked away again.
> There when the turf in springtime flowers,
>   With downward eye and gazes sad,
> Stands amid the glancing showers
>   A jonquil, not a Grecian lad.

When one recalls how this stanza is contrasted with the stanza that precedes it, nothing could be more admirable and yet spontaneous than the organization of these lines. The repeated word 'looked', the lingering of the fifth line, the effectiveness of 'downward' in the sixth line, and then the pause with the word 'stands' are all uses of language so appropriate that the lines seem to spring from the scene they describe. The same may be said of another poem in *Last Poems*, No. XXXIII, which begins:

> When the eye of day is shut,
>   And the stars deny their beams,
> And about the forest hut
>   Blows the roaring wood of dreams,
>
> From deep clay, from desert rock,
>   From the sunk sands of the main,

> Come not at my door to knock,
> Hearts that love me not again.

To the end of his life Housman could write lines which have a resilient leaping quality, like 'The blue height of the hollow roof,' in poem XV of *Additional Poems*.

Housman wrote some great poetry if not great poems and no criticism can lessen the value of certain lines and whole poems which have an independent rightness and certainty which is beyond comment. All criticism can do is to attempt to define the range of his poetry, and say whether the pessimistic philosophy which he advances repeatedly in poem after poem is an adequate attitude towards life.

Housman's poems have properties as defined as the machinery of diabolism in Baudelaire: the countryside of Western England, the lads who are brave and true, the references to the ancient world, the stilted and firmly established imperialism. Within this environment, there springs a poetry which has three main sources of inspiration: a frustrated love, a passion for justice, equally frustrated, and the view that life is misery and that man is only happy when he is safely under the ground.

Ultimately, the whole of Housman's pessimism and sense of injustice springs from the idea of frustrated love:

> He, standing hushed, a pace or two apart,
>   Among the bluebells of the listless plain,
> Thinks and remembers how he cleansed his heart
>   And washed his hands in innocence in vain.

The young, the straight, the true, the brave, gain nothing from their virtue; they are shot just the same, and the world is so vile a place that they are happiest dead: 'Let us endure an hour and see injustice done.'

This frustration is best in its purest form when it expresses a complete despair, as in 'When the eye of day is shut.' At other times it is merely suicidal, as in dozens of these poems, and at others it becomes ludicrous:

> Now in Maytime to the wicket
>   Out I march with bat and pad:
> See the son of grief at cricket
>   Trying to be glad.

Try I will; no harm in trying:
Wonder 'tis how little mirth
Keeps the bones of man from lying
On the bed of earth.

If one compares Housman's love poems with those of Donne, one sees how inadequate his rejection of love and hence life is. In Donne we feel that the poet has tasted deeply of life, and that while he is still tasting it, it turns to ashes. In Housman, we feel that he had a youthful disappointment on which he constructed an edifice of personal despair and bitterness which lasted a lifetime. For Housman himself this disappointment may have been tragic, but it is not valid as a judgement by which the whole of life, or even the life of the senses can be condemned. The effect of Donne's poetry is to make one feel that life is haunted by the sense of death and guilt; the effect of Housman's, after one has reached a certain age, merely to make one feel very sorry for Housman.

The nature of Housman's disappointment is revealed in these lines:

Because I liked you better
Than suits a man to say,
It irked you, and I promised
To throw the thought away.

To put the world between us
We parted, stiff and dry;
'Goodbye,' said you, 'forget me'.
'I will, no fear,' said I.

If here, where clover whitens
The dead man's knoll, you pass,
And no tall flower to meet you
Starts in the trefoiled grass,

Halt by the headstone naming
The heart no longer stirred
And say the lad that loved you
Was one that kept his word.

The idea of death simply as a negation of life is very strong in Housman. The idea of the city that is not, the young man who is not, the lover who is not,

---

> The pale, the perished nation
> That never see the sun,

recurs again and again in this purely negative form. For him there is just life and not-life. Death, as he points out in one of his poems, is the same as not having been born.

Death the negation of life, ill the negation of good, injustice the negation of justice, everything in Housman's poetry exists side by side in a pure and undiluted form, with the balance, of course, always on the side of the bad, because there is bound to be more death, more evil, more injustice in the world at any given moment than the reverse. He rather grudgingly admits:

> ... Since the world has still
> Much good but much less good than ill,

and in another poem, he sees everywhere the quantities of.

> Horror and scorn and hate and fear and indignation.

His puritanism is of a kind which is always very close to death not in a religious sense, like Donne or the Elizabethans, but in a pseudo-scientific sense, like Aldous Huxley's novels, simply because there is so much death and corruption about. But this means that life too ceases to be positive and becomes merely a feeble little effort to pretend, with cricket balls, footballs, sex, Shropshire, etc., that it is worth doing, when to the honest man it must be evident that nothing positive has any virtue because of the immense surplus of what is not which denies and frustrates it the whole time.

—Stephen Spender, "The Essential Housman." *Horizon* 1:4, April 1940. Reprinted in *A.E. Housman, The Critical Heritage*. Philip Gardner, ed. (London and New York: Routledge, 1992): pp. 377–380.

## KEITH JEBB ON HOUSMAN'S MYTHMAKING

[In this excerpt, Keith Jebb examines the "conjoining of sex and death" in the romance of *A Shropshire Lad*, and the way the association of death and sex relates to biblical and military motifs in Housman's poems.]

Terence Hearsay is a fictional poet in a fictional world. It may be true that this world is first presented to us in a poem about a real event, *ASL* I '1887', describing Queen Victoria's jubilee, but we are soon observing the process of the construction of a kind of microcosm. In this process, the difference between A. E. Housman and his poet, is that what Terence observes from his vantage within this mythic land is actually being created by Housman. This allows us to dispense with any notion of Housman being more intelligent or sophisticated than the Shropshire Lad: they merely exist in different dimensions. Like all created worlds this one needs its myths, and Housman very soon goes about providing them. *ASL* VIII 'Farewell to barn and stack and tree', which has Terence confronted by a man who has killed his brother, is actually a transformation of the story Cain and Abel. The unnamed Cain figure in the poem is, like his original, a "tiller of the ground", though we don't know if his victim Maurice kept the sheep (incidentally, though it may be unintended, there is certainly some irony in the note to the next poem in the book, which explains: "Hanging in chains was called keeping sheep by moonlight"). It is sometimes presumed by critics that the murderer in the poem is going to take his own life (or knows that the law will do it for him, since the next poem happens to be about a hanged man), but nothing in the poems actually tells us that. What lines like "She had two sons at rising day, / To-night she'll be alone" actually suggest, if one thinks, is the wanderings of Cain, the exile from the homeland. The difference between Housman's version of the myth and that in the Bible, is that his is a secularized rereading of it. The murderer answers to the sympathetic ear of Terence, not to the damning voice of the Lord.

The same is true of another poem based on the Bible, *ASL* XLVII, 'The Carpenter's Son.' On the literal level it is the speech—as with *ASL VIII* it is presented in inverted commas—of a man condemned to be hanged, bemoaning his fate:

> "Oh, at home had I but stayed
> 'Prenticed to my father's trade,
> Had I stuck to plane and adze,
> I had not been lost, my lads.

> "Then I might have built perhaps
> Gallows-trees for other chaps,
> Never dangled on my own,
> Had I but left ill alone."

Up to this point any resemblance to Christ's crucifixion seems incidental; while the idea of the Messiah suggesting he would have done better to make gallows for others seems blasphemous. But then Housman makes the parallel undeniable:

> "Here hang I, and right and left
> Two poor fellows hang for theft:
> All the same's the luck we prove,
> Though the midmost hangs for love."

He is dying because he could not leave 'ill' alone, but that 'ill' seems to have been love. What that love is we are not told, but then again, keeping in mind the redemptive value of Christ's death, we have the lines which end both the first and last stanzas: "Fare you well, for ill fare I: / Live, lads, and I will die". Housman's Christ will not rise from the dead; nor does he have anyone to call to from the gallows, asking them why they have forsaken him; for he belongs to a world without a God, a world created by an atheist out of the material of the Christian world in which he lived. ( ... )

A case could be made with respect to *ASL* XLIII, 'The Immortal Part', that this poem is a reworking in part of Ezekiel Chapter 37, where the Lord shows the prophet the valley full of bones and asks him, "Son of man, can these bones live?" In Housman's poem it is the bones that speak, demanding the death of the flesh:

> "When shall this slough of sense be cast,
> This dust of thoughts be laid at last,
> The man of flesh and soul be slain
> And the man of bone remain?"

Whereas in the Old Testament story the bones are reclothed in flesh, and life is called back into the dead, Housman takes the progression in reverse: death is not the removal of flesh from the bone, but the fact of having it there in the first place, since death is a continuous process of decay and "The immortal bones obey control / Of dying flesh and dying soul". It is as if the bones in the valley refused to be brought back to life, since they see themselves as the ultimate fruits of human existence:

> "Wanderers eastward, wanderers west,
> Know you why you cannot rest?
> 'Tis that every mother's son
> Travails with a skeleton."

"Travails" is an example of Housman's often-ignored verbal dexterity: not only does it include both meanings of the word—to suffer the pangs of childbirth, and to make a painful and laborious effort—but it also echoes the wandering of the previous lines with its pun on 'travels'. There is no prophet with his God to call these bones to life, and they don't need it. It becomes a myth for a godless land, a religion for the irreligious.

This mythmaking is one aspect of the creation of the Salopian universe. I have concentrated on his reworkings of Biblical material, but there are others, such as *ASL* XX, 'Oh fair enough are sky and plain', which is the story of Narcissus, already referred to in *ASL* XV. But there are other aspects to this world which Housman builds up, other recastings of reality. The military theme is one of these. It is such a strong note in the collection that Kegan Paul originally tried to persuade him to turn the book into a "romance of enlistment". Although the idea may seem absurd to us now, the words 'romance of enlistment' do adequately describe this aspect of *A Shropshire Lad*. Enlistment is both an escape and a duty, it seems; but it is an escape into death, and a duty to die. 'Reveille' (*ASL IV*) catches the note of temptation, the desire for wider horizons:

> Up, lad, up, 'tis late for lying:
>   Hear the drums of morning play;
> Hark, the empty highways crying
>   "Who'll beyond the hills away?" ( ... )

In 'Reveille' death is merely journey's end, the traveller's rest:

> Clay lies still, but blood's a rover;
>   Breath's a ware that will not keep.
> Up, lad: when the journey's over
>   There'll be time enough to sleep.

It is to clay, of course, the blood returns, a Christian reference to which Housman returns again and again, and which is especially poignant with regard to the soldier, who dies in the mud and dust of the battlefield. In 'The Recruit' (*ASL* III) death is seen more in the context of the battle, the idealised notion of battle as a fight between comrades and the enemy, where the soldier can "make the foes of England / Be sorry you were born". And here the act of dying for and among one's fellows becomes important, that one should "make the hearts of comrades / Be heavy where you die". The one true form of fellowship in the poems is the death-pact of the army, and ideas of friendship and death are never far apart:

> Far and near and low and louder
>   On the roads of earth go by,
> Dear to friends and food for powder,
>   Soldiers marching, all to die.
>
> (ASL XXXV)

It is a strange obsessive trait that friendship and death are almost always twinned. ( ... )

In *ASL* XXXIV, 'The New Mistress', the jilted lover turns to the army, as a soldier of the Queen (his new mistress on one level only). Variations on the phrase "sick am I to see you" occur in each of the four stanzas. In the first, the woman says this to her lover. In the second he says of the uniform that the Queen "will not be sick to see me if I only keep it clean". In the third, it is the sergeant who "may be sick to see me but he treats me very kind". All this playing on the phrase of rejection culminates in the final stanza: "Where the standing line wears thinner and the dropping dead lie thick; / And the enemies of England they shall see me and be sick". It is a succession of mock lovers, ending in the one he will kill or else be killed by.

I could gather examples for a long time, to prove the strength of the connection the poems forge between fellowship and death, and between love and death: because lovers in Housman's poems are, like soldiers, always dying and being replaced by other lovers. And here I would like to present something which is as close to a key to the poems as we are ever likely to get. The notion of dying for one's fellow men, which I mentioned as being important in the previous chapter, is, in fact, the covert route by which A.E. Housman's homosexuality finds expression. This may explain how death is the prime mover in the world of Shropshire; beyond the retelling of myth, beyond the martial theme (which itself occupies only half a dozen poems in *A Shropshire Lad*), beyond the theme of young love, there is death, weaving in and out of all of them. The poet and critic Stephen Spender made the comment long ago that, despite this prevalence, there is so little feeling for the dead, or curiosity about death. But he missed what actually does happen. Death is the alternative sweetheart of the poetry:

It nods and curtseys and recovers
　　When the wind blows above,
The nettle on the graves of lovers
　　That hanged themselves for love.

The nettle nods, the wind blows over,
　　The man, he does not move,
The lover of the grave, the lover
　　That hanged himself for love.
　　　　　　　　　　　　　　　(*ASL* XVI)

I quote the whole of this short poem, which is as explicit about the love/death relationship as anything the poet wrote, in the way it turns its meaning around on itself. The lovers (plural) of the first stanza hang themselves for the love of another; the singular lover of the second stanza hangs himself—it is implied by the still ambiguous "lover of the grave"—for the love of death. Yet the real heart of the poem is the seamless way that one meaning of suicide slips into the other, as if they were two sides of the same coin which flips over with the stanza-break. But do we then have to take the conjoining of sex and death (a consummation reinforced by psycho-analysis, one of whose truisms is that death is symbolic of sexual climax) and apply it to the instances when death seems bound up with the experience of male companionship?

I want to turn to *ASL* XXII:

The street sounds to the solders' tread,
　　And out we troop to see:
A single redcoat turns his head,
　　He turns and looks at me.

This single, almost incidental moment becomes epiphanic; it is a sudden meeting of two souls whose relationship will be one of total absence, but which, thanks to the luminosity of the memory, and perhaps thanks even to poetry itself, will still be a relationship:

My man, from sky to sky's so far,
　　We never crossed before;
Such leagues apart the world's ends are,
　　We're like to meet no more;

What thoughts at heart have you and I
  We cannot stop to tell;
But dead or living, drunk or dry,
  Soldier, I wish you well. ( ... )

Fascination with soldiers was not something confined to young girls, and the Guards themselves were well known in homosexual circles as a regiment where prostitutes could be found. The poem could almost be describing one of Housman's experiences in London, but such a biographical link is not necessary: what we are looking at is a hidden code within the poetry, a code which not only associates sex with death, and the desire for death, but which also seems to suggest something subtly different, namely, that (to turn a trope from the Bible) the wages of love is death. In the godless world of *A Shropshire Lad* love is forbidden, and this law will enact the inevitable separation through death. Only in death can lovers stay together, when they cannot know it:

Lovers lying two and two
  Ask not whom they sleep beside,
And the bridegroom all night through
  Never turns him to the bride.

                     (*ASL* XII) ( ... )

The only way I can read this cruel world is to go full circle, to say that the pastoral world created by A.E. Housman is in fact a metaphor for the very world in which he lived, a world where love, a certain form of love, is illegal. And, as in *A Shropshire Lad*, it 'dare not speak its name.' How deliberate the strategy was we can only guess, but what is happening seems quite clear: it is not so much that Housman was trying to write about his homosexuality without actually saying as much; what he does is create a context in which emotions that would normally have to be suppressed (and were perhaps internally repressed) can find an outlet. He could not describe Victorian society as he experienced it directly, so he reproduced it on the level of fantasy, at the same time reproducing himself within this fantasy in the figure of Terence Hearsay. What emerges is a kind of sick pastoral, shorn of ideals, idylls and any guiding principles but the arbitrary "laws of God, the laws of man".

—Keith Jebb, *A.E. Housman.* (Mid Glamorgan, England: Seren Books, 1992): pp. 80–88.

# CAROL EFRATI ON HOUSMAN'S USE OF BIBLICAL NARRATIVE

[Carol Efrati teaches English Literature at the Achva Academic College of Education in Israel. Her publications include the recently-published *The Road to Danger, Guilt, and Shame: The Lonely Way of A.E. Housman,* a close study of Housman's work in a socio-historical context, with special attention to Housman's sexuality. This excerpt examines Housman's use of Judeo-Christian biblical motifs as a narratological tool and a source of rhetorical power.]

It is a fact well known to everyone interested in the poetry of A. E. Housman that he was accustomed to take a phrase or verse from the Bible and, by slightly altering the text or the context, twist the biblical verse to his own use. Davis P. Harding and Vincent Friemarck are but two who have published studies of this technique.[1]

However, it was not only isolated excerpts which were used in this way by Housman. In a few—a very few—poems, he did precisely the same thing for complete narratives, thrice from the Old Testament and twice from the New. In each case, his treatment throws a new light on an old story as well as providing a new vantage point from which to view the poet and his work.

Housman's familiarity with the Bible can hardly be overstated. ( ... )

There are several Old Testament stories which centre on the keeping—or breaking—of orders from the Deity. The first, of course, is the story of Adam and Eve.

Adam is the original sinner, but Housman does not deal with the transgression itself. Rather, he is interested in one reason for it: discontent. This is one of the very few poems which seems to have escaped critical attention.

> When Adam walked in Eden young,
>   Happy, 'tis writ, was he,
> While high the fruit of knowledge hung
>   Unbitten on the tree.
>
> Happy was he the livelong day;
>   I doubt 'tis written wrong:

The heart of man, for all they say,
Was never happy long.

And now my feet are tired of rest,
And here they will not stay,
And the soul fevers in my breast
And aches to be away.

$(AP \text{ III})^2$

Since it was God Who created Adam and determined his nature, Adam's discontent is of the same origin as himself. God must have intended it to be part of his nature when making him.

It is on this basis that Housman questions the biblical account of life in pre-lapsarian Eden, for Adam, being the prototypical man, must have found, as all men do, that happiness is at best temporary. It was not the eating of the fruit of the forbidden tree which caused him to lose his primordial bliss; rather it was the lack of the potential for continuing contentment in primordial bliss which caused him to eat of the fruit. Housman here could never have been born. They may thus be analogous typologically to 'the fortunate fall' and therefore part of the Deity's master plan for human history.

The first thing to note, however, is that Lot is not identified by name (although the details make his identity patent despite Mortimer's confusion). Lot is simply 'He', universalized into Everyman; equally, Lot's wife is 'the woman', universalized into Everywoman. The broken commandment is likewise unspecified; it is the paradigmatic Law of God, the type of Everylaw, that 'He may keep that will and can' but 'Not I' (LP XII), nor Lot's wife, Housman's identification with the transgressor is quite clear. ( ... )

Most biblical prohibitions concern man's relationships with his society, and especially with his fellow men. Here the prohibition concerns only the relationship between man, or woman, and God, and that relationship is one of total dominance on the one side and unquestioning obedience on the other. The penalty for refusing this obedience is extreme, not 'jail and gallows and hell-fire' (LP XII) but metamorphosis into a mineral form. It is not only society that wrests individuals to its will; it is God Himself.

Let it be noted, however, that 'He' broke no commandment, and yet it is to 'his undoing' that he proceeds. Here there are many ways of reading the undertext. Both her breaking and his keeping of the law lead to 'undoing'. Since one is doomed (or saved) whether one obeys or not, it does not much matter which one does. This is pure (or impure) antinomianism and as such applicable only to avowed Christians who argue that the possession of 'grace' exempts them from moral laws. Since the subjects of the poem are not Christians, and since Housman himself rejected the foundation of Christianity (as we shall shortly see), it seems to me that the term is not applicable to this poem or to its author. In any case, this reading is not the one which seems best.

There is another way of reading the poem which seems far more satisfactory. The woman halts eternally because she has looked back. The man proceeds to disaster because he does not look back. Paralysis results from an exclusive focus on the past, what is behind in time rather than (or in addition to) space, and calamity results from the refusal to contemplate the past at all. As Professor Flieger has remarked, 'to look back with regret, like Lot's wife, is to risk losing the capacity and the will to go forward',[6] to which I would add that to go into the future without first assimilating the past is to risk losing the wisdom and experience to choose one's path wisely. In this reading, the undertext implies that 'the woman' was so tied to the past that she could not go forward, whereas the man, turning his back upon the past, could only go blindly towards his doom. To be tethered to history and to ignore it are equally good formulae for destruction. ( ... )

What the poem seems to be implying is that Lot's own actions were at least as sinful as those of the destroyed Sodomites, or alternatively as non-sinful. 'His' susceptibility to drink and sexual temptation place him on the same level as them. This susceptibility is Lot's basic nature, and it is this which is revealed on 'the hill of his undoing' where the mask of his propriety is removed. And one's basic nature can only be ascribed to one Entity: 'the God that made him' (AP XVIII).

The consequences of transgression extend not only to 'He' and 'the woman', but to the earth in general, for Sodom here is not even identified as a city. The focus is once more on the punishment, and here the brimstone which 'snowed' and the woman 'in the wilderness of salt' are linked by the common characteristic of snow and salt: their white colour. White, however, is the traditional colour of purity and innocence. The text is turned on its head by the use of colour symbolism, and the undertext by this means subtly absolves both 'the woman' and the city of guilt. If they are white, they, like

'He', are punished gratuitously. The undertext thus implies that God's justice is fundamentally flawed and unjust. If this be blasphemy, so be it.

From whatever direction we approach the lyric, we end with the same conclusion. Housman has implicitly charged a black-and-white tale of sin and punishment with a host of shades of grey; he has raised questions about both the sin and the punishment, about their relationship to each other and about their righteousness. He has replaced stark clarity with bluffed ambiguity.

The next lyric presents a textual problem. In the standard editions, it consists of seven stanzas. However, in Housman's notebooks, there is an additional stanza. Whether this is in fact part of the poem to be considered or is a separate poem fortuitously placed there cannot now be determined. When Laurence Housman prepared his brother's manuscript poems for publication, he included it as part of this work. In the Jonathan Cape edition of the *Collected Poems*, the first one-volume edition of the four separate books of poetry, and the edition on which all later editions are based, it was deleted without any real explanation by the editor John Carter (Norman Marlow believes correctly) as being in fact an independent quatrain.

Carter says, 'Closer examination made it clear that this stanza ... does not belong to this poem.'[8] However, he does not give any account of the 'closer examination' and I have been unable to discover his rationale. The verse is not included in any edition of *More Poems* after that edited by Laurence Housman, whose opinion, he perhaps having discussed the notebook material with his brother and certainly having more familiarity with his brother's mental and associational habits than any later editor could have, should not have been so lightly disregarded. I am not so sure as Carter and Marlow, and I am here replacing it, on grounds that I hope to make clear.

> When Israel out of Egypt came
>   Safe in the sea they trod;
> By day in cloud, by night in flame,
>   Went on before them God.
>
> He brought them with a stretched out hand
>   Dry-footed through the foam,
> Past sword and famine, rock and sand,
>   Lust and rebellion, home.

I never over Horeb heard
    The blast of Advent blow;
No fire-faced prophet brought me word
    Which way behoved me go.

Ascended is the cloudy flame,
    The mount of thunder dumb;
The tokens that to Israel came,
    To me they have not come.

I see the country far away
    Where I shall never stand;
The heart goes where no footstep may
    Into the promised land.

The realm I look upon and die
    Another man will own;
He shall attain the heaven that I
    Perish and have not known.

But I will go where they are hid
    That never were begot,
To my inheritance amid
    The nation that is not

*(MP* II)

[Where mixed with me the sandstorms drift,
    And nerve and heart and brain
Are ashes for the air to lift
    And lightly shower again.][9]

Structurally, the poem can be divided into a two-verse prologue (the account of the Exodus) and a series of reflections by the narrator about the personal significance of these events. The text of the 'prologue' is a straightforward, if highly condensed, account of the Exodus, the details suggesting and referring to specific incidents in the biblical account.

'Sword' refers to external opposition (both Pharaoh's armies and the forces of Amalek), 'Famine, rock and sand' suggest natural obstacles (the paucity of food and water countered by the springs issuing from the rocks, quails and manna).

'Rebellion' suggests both internal tribal unrest (the sons of Korah, Aaron and Miriam, and Aaron's sons) and Moses' own breaking of God's command, for Numbers XX.viii–xii tells that God instructed Moses to 'speak ye unto the rock ... and it shall give forth his water' but what Moses in fact did was to coerce the rock rather than address it; 'And Moses lifted up his hand, and with his rod he smote the rock twice.' The punishment for this is the heart of the story as Housman interprets it: 'And the Lord spake unto Moses ... Because ye believed me not ..., therefore ye shall not bring this congregation into the land which I have given them'[10]—'given them' but not given you. Moses cannot even hope to enter the land of the promise—although others will—and this ban provides the emotional cord linking the prophet to the poet, as we shall see.

'Lust' suggests the forbidden, pagan worship of the golden calf, associated with fertility rituals of the most obvious type. Thus, although apparently passed over in silence, the incident of the golden calf is implicit in the reference, and every single event of the Exodus is touched upon.

It is noteworthy that the manuscript[11] shows an open choice between 'rebellion' and 'idolatry'. The former can and does refer to several separate incidents not otherwise indicated; the latter can refer only to the incident of the golden calf, already present at least peripherally in the ambience of 'lust'. I suspect this was Laurence Housman's reason for opting in favour of 'rebellion', and I suspect that this would also have been Housman's final choice.

The events are not arranged chronologically but rather in a logical sequence moving inward: the active enemy, the passive opposition of nature, tribal unrest, and individual defiance and transgression. ( ... )

It is with the dying Moses that the narrator identifies himself, permitted to look upon, but forbidden to touch, the land of Canaan. In these two verses, then, we hear the voice of the dying Moses filtered through another consciousness.

It is necessary to turn to biography to understand why Housman saw in Moses an echo of himself. Like the prophet, he had glimpsed a 'promised land' which was forbidden to him by God's decree. Moses Jackson, the man he loved passionately, was as forbidden to him as Canaan was to Moses, and he, like Moses, had to content himself with the sight of what he most desired without, because of the Divine edict, being permitted to possess it. A close and enduring friendship was all that was possible. Like Moses, he too was permitted only to gaze longingly at what he was forbidden by God to possess, not in his case the physical macrocosm of the land from which he was forever divided by death but the metaphoric microcosm of his friend, beloved, longed for, forbidden by 'The laws of God, the laws of man' (*LP* XII), from whom he was forever divided by life. In this identification with the biblical Moses, Housman united himself poetically with that Moses' modern namesake.

Only after this does the focus narrow to the narrator and concentrate exclusively on him as he contemplates his own death. Unlike that of the biblical figure, his inheritance is not the living nation but 'the nation that is not', the unbegotten, the dead, the non-existent. Here, the questionable added verse both strengthens this identification of the poet/narrator with Moses and clarifies it. The non-existence he evokes consists of the dissolution of all that is essentially human ('nerve and heart and brain') and the absorption of the residue into the natural world of sand and ash, a sterile dry world of dust. ( ... )

The reading as a personal poem has been largely explored above. It need only be added that in this reading the denial of the Promised Land to the persona is a reference to his friend's marriage (giving 'ownership' of the land to 'another man') and departure from England. The gender of the legitimate 'owner' is of course appropriately shifted, as in many other poems. This gave that which he most desired (his 'promised land') to another and denied him even the consolation of almost daily contact, exiling him psychologically. ( ... )

Another man, an orthodox Christian, may perhaps attain to a Christian heaven, but not the poet who sees his 'inheritance amid / The nation that is not', that is to say the nation that is not a nation, that is in eternal exile, the people of Israel, dispersed, scorned, apparently abandoned by God, as Housman felt that he had been abandoned both by God and by Moses Jackson ('He would not stay for me to stand and gaze', *AP* VII) who are thus in a sense conflated—Moses, the 'man of God', is united on one side with Moses, Housman's personal God, and on the other side with the forsaken poet himself. In some way, Housman seems to have felt spiritually linked to the people who stood at the time as a paradigm of dispossession. ( ... )

The next poem is a denial of the very basis of Christianity itself, not the Resurrection but the Incarnation.

THE CARPENTER'S SON

'Here the hangman stops his cart:
Now the best of friends must part.
Fare you well, for ill fare I:
Live, lads, and I will die.

'Oh, at home had I but stayed
'Prenticed to my father's trade,
Had I stuck to plane and adze,
I had not been lost, my lads.

'Then I might have built perhaps
Gallows-trees for other chaps.
Never dangled on my own,
Had I but left ill alone.

'Now, you see, they hang me high,
And the people passing by
Stop to shake their fists and curse;
So 'tis come from ill to worse.

'Here hang I, and right and left
Two poor fellows hang for theft:
All the same's the luck we prove,
Though the midmost hangs for love.

'Comrades all, that stand and gaze,
Walk henceforth in other ways;
See my neck and save your own:
Comrades all, leave ill alone.

'Make some day a decent end,
Shrewder fellows than your friend.
Fare you well, for ill fare I:
Live, lads, and I will die.'

(*ASL* XLVII)

This poem, from *A Shropshire Lad*, was published by Housman himself, who took great care to disguise its true subject, as noted above. The title, ambiguous as it is, does not clearly indicate that this is a treatment of the Crucifixion. Like so many other of his titles, it is equivocal. The text is also deliberately misleading, opening the way to more than one possible (and erroneous) interpretation. The hyphenated 'gallows-tree' collapses the Victorian gallows into the Cross (the 'Tree'). 'Dangled' and 'hung' are also ambiguous, equally applicable to both modes of execution.

'Love', with its multiplicity of possible meanings, is the most ambiguous word of all. As Keith Jebb has noted, the 'ill' that the speaker could not 'leave alone' 'seems to have been love [but] what that love is we are not told.[15] ( ... )

Here we have a treatment of the Crucifixion itself. The titular character is not like Christ nor reminiscent of Christ; he is Christ. Haber, who understood this point, called the poem 'an affront to orthodoxy'[21] which of course it is, for as W. L. Phelps noted, the point of view is detached 'not only from conventional religious belief but from conventional reverence',[22] a judgment which, if non-specific, has the virtue of being to the point. Of course the approach is not conventionally pious, and Phelps at least seems to have understood what the poem was about without becoming distracted by its theological implications concerning the nature of evil.

The most nearly satisfactory reading, neatly balancing the text and the undertext, is, not surprisingly, that of Robert Graves. In his admirable essay, he calls this what it is: 'an apocryphal account of the Crucifixion' with daring, if not blasphemous, implications. By calling the Cross a 'gallows-tree' and the disciples 'lads' instead of 'brethren' or 'children', Housman sufficiently obscured the identification to produce 'the intended irony of the poem which is strewn with the plainest scriptural allusions'.[23] One of these plain scriptural references Housman uses to provide what Eugene D. Le Mire calls the crowning irony: his entreaty to men 'not to follow Him'.[24] Housman's typical turning of biblical motifs on their heads is nowhere better illustrated.

But even Robert Graves, perceptive as he is, missed what I see as the main thrust of the text. There are only two ways of regarding Christ: either he was a carpenter's son, Joshua Ben Joseph of Nazareth, or he was the son of God, the Messiah. If the latter, then in tampering with evil He indeed 'stuck' to His Father's 'trade'. But that 'trade' is specified by 'plane and adze' as carpentry rather than Godship. He indeed must be, then, what he is called in the title: the [mortal] carpenter's son and not God's. These lines only make sense as a denial of Christ's divinity. In denying the Sonship of Jesus, we have an account of the Crucifixion which also denies its theological import, making it a common execution.

To return to Jebb: 'Housman's Christ will not rise from the dead.'[25] The divine Christ is replaced by the human Joshua; the entire text is an affirmation of his merely human status, a human status emphasized by the condemned man's own words. As a man suffering human 'justice', he is as appropriate an object of sympathy as anyone incarcerated in Portland or being hung in Shrewsbury jail. This is the carefully camouflaged undertext, and carefully camouflaged it I had to be to escape even greater condemnation as the most outrageous blasphemy (at least from the Christian point of view). If in '1887' man was perhaps raised to Christhood, here Christ is lowered, or perhaps restored, to mere manhood, and there is no 'perhaps' about it. He is not 'The Carpenter's Son' but only the carpenter's son.

Let us also not forget that, recognizing the executed felon as Christ, we are dealing with the same entity whose 'laws' were responsible for the persecution of Oscar Wilde and, potentially at least, of Housman himself had his masquerade been less successful. The carpenter's son's (whether capitalized or not) attempts to combat evil loosed additional evil on the world, and as in some sense the author of persecution, it is poetic justice that he was himself persecuted. Here, from a Christian point of view, is the ultimate combination of blasphemies, all neatly enclosed in one package and so heavily masked by its wrappings that, although it makes the Christian reader distinctly uneasy, its essence, being unthinkable, is unrecognizable. ( ... )

The foregoing examination of those poems in which Housman directly handled a biblical theme suggests that he indeed identified himself with those who were in some way the victims of Divine justice as well as with those who were the victims of human 'justice' and that, in fact, he saw little difference between 'the laws of God' and 'the laws of man', which were equally unjust. His sympathies were always on the side of the 'Culprit'.

## NOTES

1. Davis P. Harding, 'A Note on Housman's Use of the Bible', *MLN* LXV (March 1950) 205–7, and Vincent Friemarck, 'Further Notes on Housman's Use of the Bible', *MLN* LXVII (December 1952) 548–50.

2. The standard abbreviations—*ASL*, *LP*, *MP* and *AP*—are used throughout. The texts are those of *A.E. Housman: Collected Poems and Selected Prose*, ed. Christopher Ricks (London: Allen Lane, The Penguin Press, 1988).

6. Verlyn Flieger, *Splintered Light: Logos and Language in Tolkien's World* (Grand Rapids, Mich.: Wm. [*sic*] Eerdmans, 1983) p. 155.

8. *The Collected Poems of A. E. Housman*, ed. John Carter (London: Jonathan Cape, 1939), 'Note on the Text,' p. 248. For Norman Marlow's acquiescence, see his *A.E. Housman: Scholar and Poet* (London: Routledge & Kegan Paul, 1958) p. 125.

9. *A.E. Housman, More Poems*, ed. Laurence Housman (New York: Alfred A, Knopf, 1936) p. 7.

10. This and other quotations from the Bible are taken from the Authorized King James version.

11. A.E. Housman, the Manuscript Remnants now in the Library of Congress, Washington DC, Item A-2, sheet 2.

15. Keith Jebb, *A.E. Housman* (Bridgend, Mid Glamorgan: Seren Books, 1992) p. 82.

21. Tom Burns Haber, 'The Spirit of the Perverse in A. E. H.', *The South Atlantic Quarterly* XL (1941) 368–78.

22. William Lyon Phelps, *The Advance of English Poetry in the 20th Century* (New York: Dodd, Mead, 1918) pp. 68–9.

23. Robert Graves, 'The Carpenter's Son', *On English Poetry* (London: William Heinemann, 1922) pp. 31–3.

24. Eugene D. Le Mire, 'The Irony and Ethics of *A Shropshire Lad*', *University of Windsor Review* I (Spring, 1965) 109–27.

25. Jebb, op. cit.

—Carol Efrati, "A. E. Housman's Use of Biblical Narrative." *A.E. Housman: A Reassessment*. (New York: St. Martin's Press, 2000): pp. 188–209.

# MASCULINE RELATIONSHIPS AND HOMOSEXUAL SUBTEXT IN HOUSMAN'S POETRY

## CRITICAL ANALYSIS OF

# *A Shropshire Lad* 15 and 44

*A Shropshire Lad* 15, "Look not in my eyes, for fear," is a rhetorical fun house, full of mirrors that distort and double; it uses irony and allusion to exaggerate these effects. In terms of its narrative and literary allusion, the first stanza of *A Shropshire Lad* 15 is a re-imagined, updated myth of Narcissus. In this version, however, the mirroring pool is replaced by the eyes of the speaker. The eye as a "limpid pool" is a familiar literary trope, as well as the conceit that "the eye is the mirror of the soul." Physically, on the retina, eyes internally mirror their object. Unlike a mirror, however, the eye is an active organ. Eyes gaze as much as they are gazed upon; when they register another's gaze, there is some emotional reaction. Thus, the eye is an image rhetorically laden with meaning, for, unlike a pool of water or a mirror, it always does more that passively and inanimately reflect an image.

"Look not in my eyes, for fear / They mirror true the sight I see"—the speaker's eyes are a potential mirror, reflecting the image of his lover. The first lines are both a warning and an invitation: "And there you find your face too clear / And love it and be lost like me" is a declaration of love. The lover's image, "contained" or mirrored in the speaker's eyes, is enthralling. It has already captivated the speaker, and he suggests that should the object of his gaze (and his affection) look into his eyes as if in a mirror, what he'll see there is an image so enticing that he will "lose himself" in that reflection—just as the speaker himself has already lost himself in the "original" image. If we go by the Narcissus myth, when the lover looks and sees his own reflection, he'll be captured there, unable to move away, and will eventually perish. Why should the lover doom himself to such a fate, the speaker asks? If the speaker is already facing such doom, as he says, this implies an interesting twist: according to the myth, the lover must also be the "mirror"—reflecting the speaker's overwhelming desire, which has enslaved him. As with the first four lines, the warning in the last two becomes an invitation to "perish" along with the speaker; "why should you as well as I / Perish?" is a rhetorical question. Moreover, to perish or "die" is another old and well-used literary trope: it is a euphemism for orgasm.

This complicated, swooning language of mirroring and captivation is all hyperbole, so unlike Housman's terse, subtle and restrained manner. Yet the second stanza's retelling of the myth in Housman's more typical style provides an ironic and more emotionally forceful counterbalance to the previous, rather unrestrained rhetoric. The speaker's inviting eyes are reduced to the inanimate pool; the lover is now the "Grecian lad" of the myth who falls in love with his own image there, and dies as a result. So the lad becomes a delicate flower, the jonquil—always gazing downward, yet now unable to see itself. Something beautiful that others may admire, the flower itself is now merely an aesthetic object, effectively inanimate.

The second stanza acts to reverse the threat and thrill of the first, where the warnings and the mirrored images were in fact declarations of desire and invitations to connect with the speaker emotionally and perhaps physically. In addition, this second stanza is a mirror in that it retells the traditional myth against the speaker's version, making the link between the poet's experience and the myth perfectly clear. Such rhetorical redundancy may seem unusual for Housman, but for *A Shropshire Lad* 15 it becomes necessary. The poem is built of doubled narratives and reflected images, yet the link between the myth and the experience is a kind of wish; for in fact they tell different stories. The inherent irony—and perhaps the futility—of this comparative effort is the subtext of *A Shropshire Lad* 15. Housman deftly employs image and allusion to convey many levels of mirrored experience, when in fact both the speaker and the "Grecian lad" are acting alone. The poem's redundancy forces it into irony. We can read in this a suggestion of alienation and isolation that reduces the panoply of images to one: the jonquil— perhaps the emotional heart of the poem, and its final image of loneliness.

In contrast, *A Shropshire Lad* 44, "Shot? so quick, so clean an ending," addresses the consequences of sexual and emotional alienation—and rejection—with straight-forward and brutal irony. This poem is about a suicide. Given Housman's usual figurations of death as an honorable, free state of being; and given death's common associations with masculine love, battle, and comradeship in his poems, suicide would seem to connote coward and effeminacy. The soldier in this poem did not die in battle, but by his own hand. Nonetheless, *A Shropshire Lad* 44 treats this particular suicide as a grim display of manly wisdom, courage, and integrity: "Oh lad, you died as fits a man."

> Oh you had forethought, you could reason
> And saw your road and where it led,
> And early wise and brave in season
> Put the pistol to your head.

Thus the poem suggests that in the soldier's (and speaker's) world, suicide is the last, most desperate, but bravest means of escape from an untenable situation, and of avoiding personal shame.

To a great extent, the poet is identifying with his subject. After the first two stanzas' validation of the soldier's suicide, how could the speaker then refer him as "the household traitor" and the "soul that should not have been born?" He is not speaking of the soldier; rather, these lines reflect personal antipathy. Homosexuality is a veiled topic in this poem; we can recognize it through the circumstances that it creates, or which surround it. For instance, the speaker refers to homosexual feeling as something beyond personal choice: "Yours was not and ill for mending" absolves the soldier of any responsibility to change himself or "mend" his ways, in that sense. However, while the topic of homosexuality remains veiled, the social consequences do not. "Dust's your wages, son of sorrow / But men may come to worse than dust." It is important to consider that shame, social alienation and whatever is worse than dust—i.e., death—were not necessary outcomes for a gay man in the late nineteenth century (although homosexual activity was not legal in Britain). This is the point at which the poet's active re-imagining of the event and identification with the soldier overwhelm both: in a sense, the suicide and the soldier disappear. What is left in their wake are the speaker's self-recriminations, and own fantasies of escape, which are all the more powerful because they are conveyed in an ironically restrained tone. There are no histrionics here, just a metaphorical "slap on the back" of the dead soldier for "biting the bullet": refusing to shame his comrades, and setting a good example for other unfortunate men in such circumstances.

Souls undone, undoing others ...
You would not live to wrong your brothers.

Many of Housman's poems convey a strong craving for masculine company; although this desire is quite often figured in terms of death, the fantasy of death does induce some degree of fulfillment in the speaker. In *Shropshire* 44, death works a bit differently. A soldier confronts the difficulties brought on by his own desire, and chooses an "ending" that will leave him "clean" and undefiled—not emotionally satisfied. The satisfaction death brings does not, as in other poems, involve the freedom to fight, live, and ultimately, to lie with other men in the grave. Rather, it is a purification, a purgation of desire. Now the solder is "Undishonoured, clear of danger / Clean of guilt ... ". Like Housman's other poems, death is a place of safety in *Shropshire* 44, but it is not a continued fantasy existence among other men—there are "no dreams, no waking." The dead soldier will never lie with his comrades in battle. A suicide, his death was isolated. Moreover, suicide is generally unacceptable in Judeo-Christian society. Although Housman himself was an avowed atheist, the historical and cultural context deserves consideration, for it too structures the soldier's response to his desire, and Housman's attitude toward the poem's subject. In this respect the soldier's desperate act ironically accentuates his—and by extension, the speaker's—social alienation, rather than patching it up with unrealizable fantasies.

Yet, as the final stanza claims, the poem itself is both an acknowledgement of this irony, and a gift. If the gift is not "worth the taking," this is perhaps because it arose out of a similar alienation, and remains as proof. Typical of Housman's work, the poem's aloof stance is inversely proportional to the speaker's emotional involvement with the subject. And *Shropshire* 44 betrays a deep and sincere sympathy with the soldier. Moreover, it is evidence of a creative, productive act that rhetorically reverses the destruction it describes. Standing in place of the dead soldier, the poem is no wreath of flowers, but a permanent, if private, sign of shared experience that "will not fade."

# *A Shropshire Lad* 15 and 44

## TOM BURNS HABER ON SHAKESPEAREAN INFLUENCES IN HOUSMAN'S FIGURATIONS OF FRIENDSHIP

[Tom Burns Haber was Professor of English at Ohio State University. He published widely on Housman in journals and has edited several collections of essays and Housman's verse. Haber's notable publications include *The Manuscript Poems of A.E. Housman; Eight Hundred Lines of Hitherto Unpublished Verse from the Author's Notebooks*, and *The Making of A Shropshire Lad: a Manuscript Variorum*. In this excerpt Haber considers Shakespeare's influence on poems that speak to masculine and love relationships in Housman's poetry.]

It might be imagined that Housman could have had no more than the ordinary reader's interest in Shakespeare's songs—one of his three admitted sources—if we thought only of some of the most popular ones, such as "Who is Sylvia?" and "Hark, hark the lark." ( ... )

### I *Songs from Shakespeare's Plays*

He appreciated the songs as being much more than lyric incidentals in the plays; he relished their indigenous dramatic values, their fidelity to the action of their contexts, their sparse accurate comment on the tragedy or comedy of a crowded scene. Housman's sympathy for "all ill-treated fellows" found congenial themes in many of Shakespeare's lyrics that express, often with typical sixteenth-century excess, the feelings of various unfortunate characters in the action of the dramas. How many of the darker traits of these lyrics and their surroundings may have entered into Housman's working imagination, no one can say; but his poetry, when we begin exploring it, offers many parallels: suicide for love, the ill conscience, innocence betrayed, the longing of age for the years of youth, the lament for the irrevocable dead. Seventeen of Housman's lyrics are devoted to the theme of the rejected lover, who ends in despair or suicide. The "lover sick to death" of *Love's Labour's Lost* (IV, iii) could meet with many of his kind in Housman's poems. ( ... )

But the strongest appeal in Shakespeare is still to be examined: the sonnets, "the most autobiographical ever written," where Housman could not fail to read, in and between the lines—so obscure to many before and since—the clear story of a predicament so like his own: the poet's anxious love of a man, the paragon of manly virtues, to whom all of his affections and desires were irresistibly drawn. Housman perceived in the poems a sensibility as acute as his own; a mind, like his, at variance with itself; passions seeking outlets he himself had been all too familiar with in his latter Oxford days. The innermost chords of his being must have been stirred by Shakespeare's declaration of his unworthiness, his abnegation of any and all claims on his friend, his despair at long stretches of absence, his assumption of all guilt in their alliance. How burningly such passages as these must have touched Housman's mind as he read or recalled the sonnets during his purgatorial period in London, when most of his poetry was written:

> Weary with toil, I haste me to my bed,
> The dear repose for limbs with travel tired;
> But then begins a journey in my head
> To work my mind when body's work's expired.
> For then my thoughts, from far where I abide,
> Intend a zealous pilgrimage to thee.... (Sonnet 27)

> 'Tis not enough that through the cloud thou break,
> To dry the rain on my storm-beaten face,
> For no man well of such a salve can speak
> That heals the wound and cures not the disgrace:
> Nor can thy shame give physic to my grief;
> Though thou repent, yet I have still the loss.
> The offender's sorrow lends but weak relief
> To him that bears the strong offense's cross. (Sonnet 34)

> How like a winter hath my absence been
> From thee, the pleasure of the fleeting year!
> What freezings have I felt, what dark days seen!
> What old December's bareness everywhere! (Sonnet 97)

> O, never say that I was false of heart,
> Though absence seemed my flame to qualify!

As easy might I from myself depart
As from my soul, which in thy breast doth lie.
That is my home of love.... (Sonnet 109)

A. E. Housman was a Victorian, not an Elizabethan, and he never addressed Moses Jackson in terms as unequivocal as Shakespeare's. Yet the essence of one of the main themes of the sonnets sounds forth from Housman's "Because I liked you better." I quote from the penciled draft (p. 207 of the first notebook), where the two-stanza poem was written; it is much more explicit than the printed text of the four stanzas of *More Poems* 31:

> Because I liked you better
>     Than friends in liking may,
> It irked you and I promised
>     I'd cast the thought away.
>
> And now the headstone naming
>     The heart no longer stirred
> Will say the lad that loved you
>     Was one that kept his word.

This exposition of one of the dominating themes of the sonnets—Time's conquest over friendship and love—is essayed frequently by Housman, again in "Smooth between sea and land" (*MP* 45) and "Stone, steel, dominions pass" (*MP* 24), and with recognizable Shakespearian overtones in *ASL* 57 (the earliest surviving draft):

> You smile today, you hearken now,
>     So sighs and griefs are over;
> You give again the lover's vow,
>     And happy is the lover.
>
> 'Tis late to hearken, late to smile,
>     But better late than never:
> I shall have lived a little while
>     Before I die forever.

The theme of the ravage of time is balanced in the sonnets by Shakespeare's proud declaration that a final victory will be his: he will defeat time and ensure his friend's immortality by enshrining him in poetry that will last forever. Housman knew the lover's anguished hatred of death, the despairing recognition that nothing can save the loved one from the supreme indignity. In *ASL* 33 (A 148, first draft) he is at the nadir of powerlessness as he contemplates the end: all he can do is to declare again his love and ask for kindness:

> If truth in hearts that perish
>     Could touch the powers on high,
> I think the love I bear you
>     Should make you not to die.
> .   .   .   .   .   .   .   .   .
> Vain care and endless longing
>     And fruitless hope to please,
> Oh, you should live for ever
>     If there were help in these.
>
> But now that all is idle,
>     To this lost heart be kind,
> Ere to a town you journey
>     Where friends are ill to find.

But another day brought another mood. Housman's self-confidence was as great in its own way as Shakespeare's ever was, and once he threw down the gauntlet to the enemy in terms like those we so often find in the sonnets. The poem was written to a youthful suicide, a person Housman never knew. He commends the act of self-destruction and ends his seven-stanza poem with this prophecy:

> Turn safe to rest, no dreams, no waking;
>     And here, man, here's the wreath I've made:
> 'Tis not a gift that's worth the taking,
>     But wear it and it will not fade. (*ASL* 44)

So much for anonymity: Housman's lyric has endowed the unknown dead with everlastingness. But that flight was not attempted again, never at his heart's supreme behest. Fancy had its limitations beyond which even love could not rise. His remorseless honesty to himself would not allow him the comfort of dallying with the surmise that he would confer immortality on Moses Jackson by engrafting him new. No wonder Housman said of his poetry that the satisfaction it gave him was something like—no more than—a mattress between him and the hard ground.

Perhaps the chief effect of the sonnets on Housman was that they encouraged him to entrust his experiences to poetry, to reach for the relief from spiritual stress that such writing often brings. What other relief offered itself to him? He must have sensed the benefice, the victory that Shakespeare, despite his prevailing pessimism, earned for himself in the reiteration that his lines, which he believed to be immortal, would endow his friend with everlastingness. Here was pride indomitable; here was certainty. It was good to study the details of another man's success, won on a hard-fought field and under conditions not unlike his own. What more natural that, when A. E. Housman unlocked his heart, Shakespeare's sonnet story, already a part of it, left its traces in *A Shropshire Lad* and the later poetry?

> —Tom Burns Haber, *A.E. Housman.* (New York: Twayne Publishers, 1967). pp. 135–146.

## ROBERT K. MARTIN ON HOUSMAN'S "TWO STRATEGIES": SEXUAL POETICS IN *A SHROPSHIRE LAD* AND *LAST POEMS*

[Robert K. Martin is Professor of English at the University of Montreal. One of the founders of academic lesbian and gay studies, he has published widely on the Bloomsbury Group, E.M. Forster, and nineteenth-century American Literature. In this essay, Martin compares Housman's different poetic "strategies" for managing and figuring the complicated demands of desire in *A Shropshire Lad* and *Last Poems*, respectively.]

This essay addresses itself to what I have called Housman's two "strategies"—two ways of responding to the situation of the homosexual through the means of his art. I identify one of these strategies with each of his volumes of poetry. The first, which I call the "strategy of survival," is the strategy of *A Shropshire Lad*; the second, which I call the "strategy of revolt," is the strategy of *Last Poems*. Although much Housman criticism treats his work as a single body, frequently even lumping all the poems into the modes of *A Shropshire Lad*, the two volumes represent very different strategies and forms of presentation of self.

Asked about his use of place, A. E. Housman replied drily, "My Shropshire, like the Cambridge of Lycidas, is not exactly a real place."[1] The remark is suggestive in several ways. It serves to remind us of *A Shropshire Lad*'s status as fiction, its qualities of invention and imagination as ways of transforming experience into art. If the "Shropshire" of the poem is not really Shropshire, neither is the speaker of most of the poems, Terence Hearsay, Housman himself. At the same time Housman's comment seems to invite us to read *A Shropshire Lad* at least partly in the light of Milton's monody. To do so is to understand much of the structure of Housman's work, the transformation of the "uncouth swain" into the "lad" of the later poem, but also to see how *Lycidas*, with its Christian reassurance, becomes an ironic model for Housman's Stoic or antitheist elegy.[2]

In the popular imagination the poems of *A Shropshire Lad* are often seen as pastoral lyrics singing the praises of innocent rural life and the loves of lads and lasses. In fact, however, the book is a series of dramatic monologues depicting a fallen pastoral. The world they portray is as cruel as Frost's rural New England—Frost is in fact one of Housman's most important spiritual and poetic descendants. The speaker gives us a panoramic view of Shropshire as a world dominated by guilt and death. And yet, paradoxically, the poems triumph over the world they record: the lads die, but the love they inspire gives rise to the poems which preserve that love in a way that life is incapable of. *A Shropshire Lad* is a book which begins in death and concludes in an eternal life of shared art and love.

*A Shropshire Lad* was indeed a deeply personal work, the poetic consequence of Housman's love for Moses Jackson and his recognition of the impossibility of fulfilling that love in life. Housman found an adequate means of rendering his love only through the effective exclusion of the personal self from the poems. Housman's invention of a rural uncouth persona was not merely an indication of his indebtedness to a poetic tradition; it was the means by which he could make his suffering into the material of art and hence surmount it. The Shropshire lad is Housman's objective correlative for his own sense of loss.

This process, which I have termed Housman's "strategy of survival," is most clearly indicated in the penultimate poem of the collection, the only one in which the speaker is specifically identified as Terence. Terence replies to accusations that his poetry (which we have just read, of course) is "stupid stuff" by explaining that his poems are not merely "a tune to dance to." If poetry is an escape from thought, then its place can well be taken by ale. But, following the liquor analogy, his brew is "sour," for it has been distilled "in a weary land," "Out of a stem that scored the hand.[3] In his first explanation of his poetry, the speaker appears to justify it in terms of reality: if his poetry is grim, it is because life is grim as well (it has, in his words, "much less good than ill").

The fourth stanza of the poem introduces a new argument, through the story of Mithridates, who uses small doses of poison to develop an immunity to it. The pain of the poems is also mithridatic; it is designed to introduce a controlled amount of pain in order that the reader may be inured against an even larger dose. By this analogy, Housman reveals his own strategy of control and distance. The king survives because he has trained his body to respond to poison; the knowledge of poison has made him strong. So, we are to understand, it is with these poems: they are also ways of learning to survive, not through escape from pain but through the ability to take the pain in small doses. As therapy for the reader, they build an immunity that may enable him to overcome adversity; as therapy for the author, they are an index of the ability of pain to heal itself, by a kind of burning-out process.

It should be remembered that the speaker in this poem is Terence—but Terence in his guise as poet, even if still the unsophisticated poet of Ludlow. The poem is thus Terence's poetics, or Housman's poetics as spoken through Terence. For Terence is integral precisely to the strategy that Housman describes in this poem. It was through the creation of a less sophisticated, cruder self that Housman could give voice to his pain while still retaining an element of control. The shepherd's lament became Housman's way of channeling, and hence mastering, his own mourning.[4] Those who met Housman were often surprised to find such an unsympathetic, cold person, not at all like the warm-hearted voice of the poems. What they seem not to have understood is the extraordinary inner tension that led to the creation of two different public identities, the cruelly correct classics scholar, and the lively, vulgar lad. Housman seems to have had no way of bringing them together.

The Mithridates poem bears great weight, but it is not the last poem in the collection. For a final work, following his poetic justification, Housman wrote a kind of envoi, for which he returned to his characteristic ballad (or hymn) meter. "I hoed and trenched and weeded" no longer justifies the poetic method, but accepts simultaneously its unfashionable quality and its ultimate survival. As the opening line makes clear, the speaker is still very much a rural figure, but his personality is no longer at issue. Here it is the horticultural metaphor itself which is central. For the poems are flowers which go unsold at the fair, since their "hue" is "not the wear."[5]

Since they are flowers, they also contain the means of their own continuation. The poet sows their seeds so that they may flower again another year. By this capacity for regeneration, they are able to survive the poet himself. In miniature form (four quatrains of common meter), the poet thus presents an account of his own life and art. The speaker makes an offering of his love and labor, but it goes "unheeded." He then "sows" the seeds of his first offering, which is to say, he creates the poems that are the product, or seed, of the love once proffered and refused. That seed will yield new flowers and come to adorn "other luckless lads." It is important to note here that in this poem, more than any other of this collection, Housman is open about the homosexual meanings of his heritage: the flowers that he sows are to be worn by other lads. In that way his own love, so hopeless and so painful, becomes a source of hope and comfort. For the love, once transformed into art, is able to transcend time and prejudice until it finds its rightful place.

The analogy of the sower and the seed echoes, especially in lines 9 and 10, "Some seed the birds devour, / And some the season mars," the Gospel of St. Matthew, 13, where Jesus explains his own method of speaking in parables. The allusion thus functions two ways: it signals Housman's transformation of his source and his use of his poems as an analogue to the Word, it also signals to us Housman's own parabolic method. The poem is not realistic; instead it translates the poet's work into the language of the country and then by revealing its source back into its origins as a parable about the survival of language. Like the Whitman of the "Calamus" poems, which seem remarkably close to this poem, the speaker concludes by withdrawing, leaving only his work, seen as flower seed or leaf of grass, behind. Nature subsumes the artist and preserves his creation until a time when it may find response. Housman's work is therefore a parable, not only in the obvious sense that the flowers here are a metaphor, but in the sense that it is cast as a message in a secret tongue. The male love which gave rise to the poems would survive in them until it could flower again.

The idea that art preserves by transforming love from the transitory realm of the real into the eternal world of the imagination was not unique to Housman, of course, although it is one of his most persistent themes. There is perhaps no more important source for this concept as expressed in Housman's poetry than in Shakespeare's sonnets, such as sonnet 18, with its lines,

> But thy eternal summer shall not fade
> Nor lose possession of that fair thou owest;
> Nor shall Death brag thou wander'st in his shade,
> When in eternal lines to Time thou growest:
>> So long as men can breathe or eyes can see,
>> So long lives this and this gives life to thee.

Housman's most famous single poem, "To an Athlete Dying Young," is one of a number of his poems which touch on this theme. It must be remembered that the poem is based on Pindar's Olympian Odes and that, like them, it celebrates the beauty and grace of the athlete at the moment of his perfection. It is therefore inaccurate to think of Housman's elegiac poems in terms of the world-weariness and *amour de l'impossible* of the poets of the '90s: for their mourning is always countered by an assurance of a compensating life, never certainly in the Christian terms of *Lycidas* but often in the aesthetic terms of Shakespeare.

"To an Athlete Dying Young" is structured around the figure of the laurel, which, as Housman knew, was used for the wreath of the victorious athlete and for the poet. Although the laurel in the poem refers explicitly only to the athlete's crown, the poem's full meaning depends upon an understanding of its unstated other reference. For the poem itself is the laurel wreath bestowed on the young man, and it is the wreath which guarantees a life beyond death. In the third stanza, the speaker praises the youth:

> Smart lad, to slip betimes away
> From fields where glory does not stay
> And early though the laurel grows
> It withers quicker than the rose.

In the natural world, indicated by the "fields where glory does not stay," nothing is permanent, all life leads to death. The laurel grows "early" because the beauty of the youth achieves its peak, according to the Greek ideal of beauty, in late adolescence. But that beauty dies equally quickly, and indeed "withers quicker than the rose," the emblem of feminine beauty as well as of short flowering.

The final stanza returns to the figure of the laurel, now transformed from an emblem of early death into one of permanent life:

> And round that early-laurelled head
> Will flock to gaze the strengthless dead,
> And find unwithered on its curls
> The garland briefer than a girl's.

The irony of this transformation, that this garland which is "briefer than a girl's" should be still "unwithered," is the poet's assertion of the permanence of art (and memory). For although the athlete is presumably dead, he is always imagined in the poem's terms as alive (indeed the title sees him only "dying," not dead): the imperatives of stanza 6 "set" and "hold" suggest his continued activity, while it is the others who are now "the strengthless dead." He remains alive because he wears a laurel that will not wither, a garland of words, in fact the very poem we are now reading and in that act gazing once more on that "early-laurelled head." Thus the poem's last line, "The garland briefer than a girl's," accomplishes an ironic triumph, since its very brevity is what enables it to survive; so too the line suggests the love for a young man, although destined for an early death, prevails over death in a way that the rose garland of heterosexual love cannot. Like most pederastic poems of this period, Housman's "To an Athlete Dying Young" suggests that it is the purity of boy-love which preserves it from time and mortality.[6]

Although "To an Athlete" does not explicitly identify the garland of the last line as a trope for the poem, there can be no doubt that this was Housman's intention, for he used the same figure in a closely related poem, *A Shropshire Lad* 44, "Shot? so quick, so clean an ending?" There can be few readers who are not moved by this expression of self-hatred. Did Housman really prefer death before "dishonour"? The poem poses many problems, not the least of which is its tone. It seems certain that the young cadet (about whose suicide Housman had read) aroused a sentiment similar to that which the athlete produced. Reading of this young man and his death, Housman chose to preserve him from the anonymity of time by transforming him from pathetic victim to hero. Thus much of what the poem accomplishes is subversive: a suicide is praised as if he were a military hero (he is "brave," "wise," and "right"), and his death becomes the means of new life. For it is the poet's act of love, his response to the unknown cadet, that creates the laurel of the last stanza:

> And here, man, here's the wreath I've made:
> 'Tis not a gift that's worth the taking,
> But wear it and it will not fade. ( ... )

## II

If the fundamental strategy of *A Shropshire Lad* is the attempt to overcome pain by controlling it, Housman's second (and final) collection of poems, *Last Poems*, proposes a very different strategy. These are poems of rebellion, poems that clearly affirm life over death. For whatever reason, Housman appears no longer to have found necessary the strategies that made *A Shropshire Lad* possible. Most of the poems appear still to be written in the voice of Terence (although there are striking exceptions such as the "Epithalamium," which Housman wrote for Moses Jackson's wedding), but the dominant elegaic tone is gone. Indeed the first poem sets the tone for the volume by insisting on a refusal of death. Housman was in his 60's when the book was published, and so one might have anticipated poems which looked toward the end. Instead the book is dominated by its *carpe diem* theme; the presence of death makes life all the more valuable. In the initial poem, "The West," the speaker acknowledges the appeal of death, troped variously as the West, the sea, and "our native land." If there is still no reason to deny that all life will terminate in death, yet there is no reason to succumb to its beguilements. The reason for the change is clear in the poem: the presence of the comrade who "stride for stride, / Paces silent at my side." The word "lad" is used twice in the poem, both times in association with the desire for death, while the living figure is referred to four times as "comrade." The use of these terms in this way appears to signal a shift from the pederastic mode to the Whitmanic mode. There is a strong sense of a newfound equality that matches the determination to accept life, to "Plant your heel on earth and stand." Since death will mean an end to love, the call of the poems is to life:

> When you and I are spilt on air
> Long we shall be strangers there:
> Friends of flesh and bone are best:
> Comrade, look not on the West. ( ... )

One of the best known poems from this collection, "The chestnut casts his flambeaux," is indicative of the change in attitude. The poem's sense of loss through time is carefully controlled by the ironic voice. His plaints may be those of a slightly drunk Terence, but the anger is now present along with the self-pity, particularly in the curse against "Whatever brute and blackguard made the world." It is a cry like that in *Atalanta in Calydon*, against a malevolent god. Shorn of hope for an afterlife, man in these poems has only the possibility of assuming human responsibilities, those which require him to do his work as best he can. The Stoic philosophy of the poem is slightly undercut by the final phrase, "and drink your ale," but it remains nonetheless essential to Housman's attempt to delineate a world without god. He seeks no consolations, but indeed uses the confrontation with evil and absence as the occasion for spiritual growth. Man is, as poem 12 puts it, "a stranger and afraid / In a world [he] never made."

Although Housman's rejection of Christianity appears to have occurred fairly early in his life (it became final around 1880–1881) and although it is in any case not unlike that of Swinburne in its angry phase or Arnold in its milder moments, in this particular poem Housman seems to draw a connection between his "criminality" and his atheism. It is important to recall the crimes and criminals of *A Shropshire Lad*, and to suggest that they may be, more than realistic portrayal, the metaphor for Housman's own situation as a sexual criminal, an awareness heightened for him, of course, by the Wilde trial. In the earlier volume the representation of his own sexuality as crime remained at the level of metaphor; it requires a knowledge of biography to guess that Maurice's murderer in *A Shropshire Lad* 8 may represent to some extent Housman's own outlawed status as a homosexual. In *Last Poems*, however, the feelings of anger are much closer to the surface. "Let them mind their own affairs," the speaker declares, or "look the other way."

> But no, they will not; they must still
> Wrest their neighbour to their will,
> And make me dance as they desire
> With jail and gallows and hell-fire.

The poem effectively dramatizes the mingling of religious and civil sanctions, all in the name of a superficial conformity on a matter that is none of "their" affair. By choosing the metaphor of the dance,

Housman emphasizes the triviality of the difference and the sense of disproportion between the "crime" and the punishment. At the same time, the metaphor of the "stranger" and the "foreign laws" suggests the depth of Housman's alienation and his recognition that he would always live in a world that he could never be fully a part of.

NOTES

1. B. J. Leggett, *Housman's Land of Lost Content: A Critical Study of A Shropshire Lad* (Knoxville: Univ. of Tennessee Press, 1970), p. 92, quoting from Cyril Clemens, "Some Unpublished Housman Letters," *Poet Lore* 53 (1947), 262.

2. Housman's "A Winter Funeral" is the best example of this.

3. This line seems to have had an influence on Hardy: see 1.5 of "The Darkling Thrush," written in 1900.

4. The importance of the persona is discussed by B. J. Leggett, *The Poetic Art of A. E. Housman: Theory and Practice* (Lincoln: Univ. of Nebraska Press, 1978), p. 49. But he carefully avoids any connections to Housman's life: whatever the "private compulsions," he argues, the "poet's own emotional life, however fascinating, is at present beyond the range of criticism" (p. 53). This attitude is typical of Housman criticism: F. W. Bateson writes, for instance, "a critic's first concern is with the poems as poems and not with the neuroses of his poet" ("The Poetry of Emphasis," in Christopher Ricks, ed. , *A. E. Housman: A Collection of Critical Essays* [Englewood Cliffs: Prentice-Hall, 1968], p. 131.) No one seems to consider the possibility that the "private" life will be given shape in the art.

5. The choice of the color metaphor is interesting, especially in connection with Housman's poem, unpublished during his lifetime, on the Wilde trial, "Oh who is that young sinner with the handcuffs on his wrists?" in which it is the "colour of his hair" that leads to the sentence of hard labor. It may be linked to the persistent association of certain colors with homosexuality, such as yellow, green, or lavender. The Wilde poem is discussed by Joseph Cady, "Housman and the Struggle for a Homosexual Voice," unpublished paper delivered at MLA, 1976.

> —Robert K. Martin, "A.E. Housman's Two Strategies: *A Shropshire Lad* and *Last Poems.*" *The Victorian Newsletter* 66 (1984): pp. 14–15, 16–17.


# RUTH ROBBINS ON THE "CURIOUS CONSTRUCTIONS" OF MASCULINITY IN HOUSMAN AND WILDE

[Ruth Robbins is a senior lecturer in literary studies at University College, Northampton. She is the author of *Victorian Gothic: Literary and Cultural Manifestations in the Nineteenth Century*. In this excerpt, Robbins considers the means by which masculinity and "manliness" were constructed historically, legally, and poetically, in the writing of Oscar Wilde and A.E. Housman.]

Wilde's *The Sphynx* (1894) and A. E. Housman's *Shropshire Lad* collection (1896) [ ... ] fall either side of a temporal boundary: April and May 1895, the dates of the trials and imprisonment of Oscar Wilde. Wilde's trial may be understood as the end of an era,[3] and in that sense the dates of the two poems may be said to have a particular cultural significance. I conclude with a discussion of Wilde's poetic response both to his own disgrace, and to Housman's poetry, *The Ballad of Reading Gaol* (1897). ( ... )

In the trial, it was the discourse of poetry which provided the index of a 'criminal' sexuality. The poetry of Wilde and Housman may be seen as different but comparable models for the construction of masculinity in the run up to and aftermath of the events of April and May 1895. Both were trying to articulate same-sex love, the love that dare not speak its name, via the strategy of a poetic code. An example of how the classification of discourse was used in the proceedings is the way that a letter written by Wilde to Lord Alfred Douglas was used as one of the key pieces of evidence. The letter had been used in an attempt to blackmail Wilde by the renters patronized by himself and Douglas.

> My Own Boy, Your sonnet is quite lovely, and it is a marvel that those red rose-leaf lips of yours should have been made no less for music of song than for madness of kisses. Your slim gilt soul walks between passion and poetry. I know Hyacinthus, whom Apollo loved so madly, was you in Greek days.

Wilde signed off, 'Always, with undying love, yours, Oscar'.[5] At the trial, Wilde described how this letter was open to more than one interpretation. Carelessly left in the pocket of an old suit of clothes by Douglas, it had been used to try to extort money from Wilde. The blackmailer, William Allen, had commented to Wilde that 'a very curious construction can be put on that letter'; but in his account of this affair at the first trial, Wilde told how he had replied that 'The letter, which is a prose poem, will shortly be published in sonnet form in a delightful magazine, and I will send you a copy of it.'[6] The response was a typical Wildean move. Allen clearly meant the letter could be constructed as evidence of criminal congress between Wilde and Douglas; at best it represented an example of linguistic effeminacy; at worst, it 'proved' homosexual activity. Wilde's response was intended to turn the tables on his interlocutor. Poetry, after all, is an art which encourages curious constructions to be put on it, and in terms of Wilde's own theories of art, that meant that the responsibility for meaning was finally to be located with the recipient rather than the originator: 'Those who find ugly meanings in beautiful places are corrupt without being charming. This is a fault.'[7] ( ... )

Wilde was not, of course, only convicted on the basis of the letter. But its appearance at the trial is nonetheless significant, as is his defence of it to Allen that it was a poem. Part of Wilde's 'guilt' resided in the fact that he refused to take seriously the threat that a curious construction could be put on the letter. ( ... )

How does a man write in such a way as to ensure that his audience is in no doubt about his 'manliness'? There is no precise formula, but the choices of form and matter, the how and the what in writing, and the context in which the writing takes place, provide some clues. They must be chosen in order to reflect the expected virtues of masculinity, now being defined not as adult qualities, but in opposition to femininity. ( ... )

In 1894, Oscar Wilde published in book form a poem which he had probably begun as early as 1874: the poem was illustrated by Charles Ricketts and dedicated 'To Marcel Schwob in Friendship and Admiration'. Its title was *The Sphynx*. Wilde was at this point reaching the height of his powers and his fame, and although the conception of the poem was twenty years old—the prentice work of a young student—he must nonetheless have believed that it was still relevant to his more mature aesthetic concerns.

The poem narrates the variety of moods and associations evoked by a statuette (or paperweight) in the mind of its impressionable student owner. The sphynx's perverse shape—a form which is *between* woman and beast—inspires a massive range of ideas; historical, geographical, philosophical and sensual. It permits the poetic persona to travel as far as possible from the exigencies of the here and now. It is a poem about contrasts and opposites, in which the persona's relative youth ('I have scarcely seen some twenty summers') is placed in opposition to the sphinx's ancient wisdoms and experience: 'A thousand weary centuries are thine.' His sensual proximity to this mythological creature will enable him to gain a privileged access to her past. Through her he will see the affairs of Antony and Cleopatra and of Venus and Adonis; he will see the flight of the Holy Family, and the love of Hadrian and Antinous. Touching her ('put your head upon my knee! / And let me stroke your throat') will put him in touch with the wealth of sexual experiences, both bizarre and perverse, which may have been hers:

> Did giant lizards come and crouch before you on the reedy banks?
> Did Gryphons with great metal flanks leap on you in your trampled couch?
> Did monstrous hippopotami come sidling towards you in the mist?
> Did gilt-scale dragons writhe and twist with passion as you passed them by?

These speculations continue to include lovers in more human and then in godly shapes, until he decides that the only worthy lover for her must have been Ammon, or the Libyan Jupiter.

The pleasure of speculation is eventually worn out. The poetic persona first finds himself subject to a decadent ennui, a weariness with the products of his own imagination. Then ennui becomes disgust and fear. The sphinx's major quality is her durability, but the poet becomes bored with her 'thousand weary centuries', and begins to seek closure through death. As far as he can remember, 'only one God has ever died. / Only one god has let His side be wounded by a soldier's spear.' He returns from the pagan to the Christian, and begs to be left to his crucifix.

*The Sphinx* is a poem about and of deferral. The arcane vocabulary defers the reader's extraction of meaning: the inordinately long, internally rhymed lines dramatize deferral, putting off closure. The poem enacts a contradiction—it shows the frenzy which the poet's imagination has engendered, whilst at the same time demonstrating that the frenzy cannot be resolved. There are no limits left to transgress. Whilst the form of the poem exemplifies excess (it overspills its meter), the content crosses boundaries of decency, to the extent that a pagan sensual experience becomes enmeshed with a spiritual one with the entrance of Christ into the poem. But Christ does not bring the release of satisfied desire since the poet only calls on him out of exhaustion. The arousal is never resolved; it can only, in this context, lead to increased arousal. As Regenia Gagnier suggests, *The Sphynx* 'is a textbook-complete catalogue ... of polymorphous perversity. The poem is a poem of excess in the sense that the object of desire is technically absent; the desire compulsively flows from the subject's brain.'[23] The absence of the object of desire means of course that the only outlet for that desire is linguistic. The poet only talks himself to a standstill, using words to replace the actions which they describe, and which he would like presumably to enact. Instead of having adventures like Allan Quatermain, the poet merely talks about them. And since language is his only outlet, and since the actions which he wants to perform are in a sense 'unspeakable' and excessive, then so too are the words in which he expresses himself. This language has nothing to do with efficiency of communication; in the substitution of words for deeds, the poem is insisting only on the pleasure of words, to which extent, the poem is, like the courtroom letter, phatic.

The poem however, unlike the letter and indeed much of Wilde's other literary work, did not form part of the evidence against him at his trials. On the other hand, it does share many of the features of the texts which were used as evidence of his guilt. Like the letter, and like *Dorian Gray*, it gives voice to actions which should be neither spoken nor performed. And in a context in which, as Frank Mort has argued, all sexual pleasure was referenced as '*sexual immorality*',[24] the 'love that dares not speak its name' was the most immoral of possible forms. Wilde did dare to speak the name of sexual pleasure, and got away with it until the point where the word and the deed were 'proved' by a court of law to be intimately connected. Revenge was exacted not only on his person, but also on his plays, which were swiftly withdrawn from the theatres. The linguistic pleasure which he took in his creations, and which he invited his audience to share, was harmless whilst ever it was not understood. Whilst he could rely on the ignorance of an audience who could not find 'ugly meanings in beautiful things', the literature was more or less safe; the link between sexual and textual significance could be ignored. But once prove the relationship between the two and not only is the writer implicated, but so is the reader. Reading Wilde meant that one had shared his transgression of the limits of decency.

On 25 May 1895 Oscar Wilde was found guilty under 'the 11th section of the Criminal Law Amendment Act [1885], and sentenced to two years penal servitude'.[25] Wilde served his sentence, relieved only by one or two special privileges (he was, for example, eventually allowed to read and write in his cell) and by the visits of his very few remaining friends, including the most faithful of them all, Robert Ross. It is said that during these visits, Ross recited to Wilde some of the poems from A. E. Housman's *A Shropshire Lad*, which had been published in March 1896, and which Ross had learned by heart to offer to his friend.[26] As visits were both rare and short, and closely policed, Ross must have felt very strongly about these poems.

It is difficult to think of a greater contrast than that of the poetry of Wilde and Housman. Where Wilde is verbose, pleasure-seeking, list-making and adventurous in form and substance, Housman is restrained, restricted, seemingly loyal to the landscape and the Romantic poetic traditions of England. *A Shropshire Lad*, though not an immediate success, received a range of favourable responses in the press; the reviewer for *The Times*, 27 March 1896, commented that Housman had struck 'a decidedly original note', and that he had a gift for 'melodious expression'. R. P. Graves quotes at length the review which apparently gave Housman the most pleasure, in which Hubert Bland praised Housman's achievement of an 'essentially and distinctively new poetry' where the 'individual voice rings out true and clear'. *A Shropshire Lad* represented the 'direct expression of elemental emotions, of heart-thoughts', and was only at fault inasmuch as the poems lacked 'gladness'.[27]

The beauty of the verse was, however, only one of Ross's likely motives for introducing it to Wilde. For the poems not only have a lyric beauty, but they also contain a strategy, which Ross may have hoped that Wilde would be able to use as well, for negotiating between the sincere expression of emotion and the public's sense of decorum. Thus, though Housman shares Wilde's fascination with youth and male beauty, his poems are so tightly controlled that any message is only just stated, and is never expanded. In *The Sphynx* Wilde had contrasted his own youth with the sphinx's wealth of experience, but his youth was not an index of his own innocence. His poem feels extravagant and exuberant. In utter contrast, Housman narrows the field. In the second of the collection's poems, he too claims to be only twenty: 'Now of my threescore years and ten, / Twenty will not come again.' But the urgency of the sense of time passing is not expressed by the need to have and to write many experiences; rather, Housman's persona only wants to have the same emotion over and over again:

> And take from seventy springs a score,
> It only leaves me fifty more.

And since to look at things in bloom
Fifty springs is little room,
About the woodlands I will go,
To seek the cherry hung with snow.

Housman limits his scope for emotion in a poetic form whose very vocabulary and structure is pared to the minimum. Where Wilde's lines spilled over in the excitement of what they were saying, Housman's are quite rigorously end-stopped by the strength of mostly monosyllabic rhymes. The effect is that of the seeming simplicity of verse written for children. It conveys an impression of innocence which is in complete opposition to Wilde's 'experience' and 'guilt'. The poem is also conceptually limited. The urgency of passing time is expressed in a vocabulary which is both small and 'ordinary'. It is rooted in the solidity of its woodland surroundings by the words which describe them: trees, cherry, bloom, bough and woodland. The second stanza does take us away from the wood into a more abstract concept of time, but the return to the landscape is immediate and complete, so that the first and last stanzas are virtually mirror-images of each other, where the poet returns to the 'cherry hung with snow' which in the first stanza had been the 'loveliest of trees ... Wearing white for Eastertide'.

The argument continues as to whether Housman was technically as guilty as Wilde under section 11 of the Criminal Law Amendment Act, but his 'emotional guilt' can scarcely be doubted. 'As everyone knows, Housman's thing had more to do with slaughtered soldiers, Shropshire rough trade and luxuriant misery' than with 'the heart of man', comments Francis Spufford. At Oxford he had met the athletic and brilliant Moses Jackson, 'who went off to become a rather ordinary married headmaster in India, while Housman spent the rest of his days carving "AEH 4 MJ" into every poetic tree-trunk he came across.'[28] Spufford is, of course, wrong. Not everybody knew. Some suspected and others, probably including Ross, guessed: not even Housman's homosexual brother, Laurence, was made the repository of a positive disclosure, though 'he would certainly have received a sympathetic hearing' in that quarter.[29] It was really only after Housman's death (in 1936) that his sexual preferences became widely 'known'.

What is clear from a reading of *A Shropshire Lad* is that even if Housman had stood trial as Wilde did, it is most unlikely that his poetry could ever have formed part of the evidence against him. As Neil Bartlett has pointed out, *The Oxford English Dictionary* defines love as being 'that feeling of attachment which is based upon difference of sex ... used specifically with reference to love between the sexes.' Bartlett wonders if the editor had known what he was doing 'when he cited a quotation from ... *A Shropshire Lad* as one of his authorities on the subject: "*Oh when I was in love with you, then was I clean and brave.*'" [30] It is a rhetorical question, but the answer must surely be 'no', given that the L-section was completed between 1901 and 1903, too soon after the Wilde trials for open sympathy with same-sex love to be expressed in a work which literally defined English(ness).

The keyword which defines Housman's poetry is restraint, and this may be one reason why his poetry would not have landed him in court. It never overtly transgresses any limits. The judge at Wilde's trials spoke of sexuality periphrastically ('the crime of which you stand convicted') and impersonally. He used the impersonal pronoun 'one' to represent his withdrawal from the arena of possible corruption. Housman's poetry shares that circumspection. Wilde, we might say, was convicted at least in part on a premise of his own making. If he argues, following Pater, that life reaches its highest achievement when it is lived as art, he should not have been surprised when his own art was used against him as evidence of his life. In crossing the boundary between separate spheres, he found that the interpretations of the one were the same as the interpretations of the other. Housman on the other hand, maintained what Christopher Ricks has called a *cordon sanitaire* between his poetry and the rest of his life. [31] In his lecture, 'The Name and Nature of Poetry', delivered towards the end of his life in 1933, Housman was very clear on the dangers involved in mixing up life with art: 'Experience has taught me, when I am shaving of a morning, to keep watch over my thoughts, because, if a line of poetry strays into my memory, my skin bristles so that the razor ceases to act.' He goes on to suggest that poetry 'goes through me like a spear'. [32] Mixing poetry with practicality for Housman seems to have involved endangering the physical wellbeing of his person. He therefore took the decision to police his own boundaries and to enact a radical separation of the different aspects of his life.

This decision does find its way into the poetry in that *A Shropshire Lad* is informed largely by a fear of emotional commitment. Love is consistently lost or sacrificed. The innocent enthusiasm of 'Loveliest of Trees' is repeatedly betrayed; only the love of nature is a love without risk—all other forms of attachment will be disappointed. There is, however, a price to be paid for the refusal to engage in life, and it is better to live a little than to die entirely without experience into the night where 'the bridegroom ... never turns him to the bride'. The poems cannot decide whether the risk is worth it. And in poem XV the fear of involvement is explicitly the fear of same-sex love. The poem warns against love, but not the love of opposites, man and woman; the danger is to be found in the love of the same by the same, imaged as the love of one's own reflection:

> Look not in my eyes, for tear
>   They mirror true the sight I see,
> And there you find your face too clear
>   And love it and be lost like me.
> One the long nights through must lie
>   Spent in star-defeated sights,
> But why should you as well as I
>   Perish? gaze not in my eyes.
> A Grecian lad, as I hear tell,
>   One that many loved in vain,
> Looked into a forest well
>   And never looked away again.
> There, when the turf in springtime flowers
>   With downward eye and gazes sad,
> Stands amid the glancing showers
>   A jonquil, not a Grecian lad.

For Housman there is always a choice between action and contemplation, between life and art. But whatever decision is taken, it is not final or universal. Each solution is limited only to the context in which it appears. Sometimes the speakers attempt to evade the choice altogether, as in Poem XXX: 'Others, I am not the first, / Have willed more mischief than they durst'; but this option is illusory since the speaking subject is tortured even in the grave by the fire and ice which represent the choice that he has not made:

> But from my grave, across my brow
> Plays no wind of healing now,
> And fire and ice within me fight
> Beneath the suffocating light.

At other times, it is the suicide's choice which is praised:

Shot? so quick, so clean an ending?
  Oh that was right, lad, that was brave:
Yours was not an ill for mending,
  'Twas best to take it to the grave.

The suicide has the speaker's envy for having made a decision which is so final, and for having found a method for achieving utter unconsciousness: 'Turn safe to rest, no dreams, no waking.' Another variant is the choice of an unthinking life where unconsciousness is achieved through camaraderie—'jesting, dancing, drinking' (XLIX)—favoured because it is thought which is dangerous to a man's wellbeing: ''tis only thinking / Lays lads underground.'

Housman shared with Wilde the theme of world-weariness. Sometimes he spoke it directly, sometimes he dramatized it in poems which evince a sympathetic identification with the alienated—the enlisted soldier, the criminal, the betrayed lover and the suicide. He, like Wilde, uses their alienation to speak of his own, but unlike Wilde, this is a heavily coded message which does not immediately invite a 'curious construction' to be placed upon it. As Julia Kristeva has argued 'poetic language is a "double"' in which it is impossible to arrive at absolute definitions of the meaning of truth. Poetry is double in its division of the writing subject into a subject of enunciation and a subject of utterance, which may be rewritten as the 'real' source of the narrative—the writer—and its ostensible source within the text, the character constructed out of, or by, the writer to speak his or her words.[33] But there are degrees of doubleness, degrees of difficulty in sorting out the relationships between the real and the ostensible speakers of a poem's words. Housman's poems appear to invite only the simplest forms of poetic pleasure, those of familiar stanza forms, unpretentious rhythms and easy rhymes. A reader would have to work at being shocked or dazzled by *A Shropshire Lad*—unless, that is, (s)he was 'in the know' about the code which Housman was using. There is evidence of the collection's homoerotic content. There is the succession of young male speakers and more particularly, the prevalence of soldiers amongst them: and soldiers were well-documented as having semi-professional careers as prostitutes alongside their more 'manly' duties. The soldier is a particularly double image and represents the claims of both an acceptable and dominant code, and the subversive potential of counter-cultural voices.[34] For those with access to the code, the insistent reference to young male persons as 'lads' might have been evidence too: it emphasizes both maleness and youth, the twin reference points of the homoerotic. (Wilde's equivalent term was 'boy', as it is used in the letter to Douglas, and on which the prosecution commented unfavourably at his trial.[35]) Housman's insistent combination of pleasure for the moment with his overwhelming sense of the possibly fatal consequences of pleasurable actions is another indicator. (The majority of the poems were, after all, written in the first five months of 1895, including the period of the Wilde trials: 'From Wenlock Edge he could see as far as Reading Gaol', wrote Desmond MacCarthy.[36]) But Housman's poetry allows all these things to be read 'straight'; it invites the readings acceptable to dominant cultures at least as much as it invites counter-cultural readings. And in the context of the immediate aftermath of the Wilde trials, it would have been a brave reviewer indeed who would insist on the doubleness of possible readings of *A Shropshire Lad*. To do so would be to admit that the reader had himself access to the code, knew how to speak 'the love that dare not speak its name'. Housman had found a way of not calling a spade a spade, whilst still leaving sufficient clues for the initiated to follow his alternative meanings.

## NOTES

3. See the introduction to *Fin de Siècle/Fin du Globe: Fears and Fantasies of the Late Nineteenth Century*, ed. John Stokes (Macmillan: Basingstoke, 1992), p. 1, and John Stokes, *In the Nineties* (Hemel Hempstead: Harvester Wheatsheaf, 1989).

5. *The Selected Letters of Oscar Wilde*, ed. Rupert Hart-Davis (Oxford and New York: Oxford University Press, 1979), p. 107.

6. Richard Ellmann, *Oscar Wilde* (Harmondsworth: Penguin, 1988), pp. 419–20.

7. Oscar Wilde, Preface to *The Picture of Dorian Gray* (1891), ed. Peter Ackroyd (Harmondsworth: Penguin, 1985), p. 21.

23. Regenia Gagnier, *Idylls of the Marketplace: Oscar Wilde and the Victorian Public* (Stanford: Stanford University Press, 1986), p. 45.

24. Frank Mort, *Dangerous Sexualities: Medico-Moral Politics in England since 1830* (London and New York: Routledge, 1987), p. 37.

25. Holbrook Jackson, *The Eighteen Nineties* (1913) (London: The Cresset Library, 1988), pp. 95–6. Eighteen years or so after the event, Jackson seems to have accounted it prudent not to name in so many words what Wilde had done.

26. See Richard Perceval Graves, *A. E. Housman, The Scholar-Poet* (Oxford: Oxford University Press, 1981), p. 113; and John Stokes, *In the Nineties* (New York and London: Harvester Wheatsheaf, 1989), p. 109.

27. Graves, *A. E. Housman, The Scholar-Poet*, pp. 112–13.

28. Francis Spufford, 'Those ruthless rhymes and rotten lads', review of Housman's poems by John Bayley, *The Guardian*, 6 July 1992, p. 25.

29. Norman Page, *A. E. Housman, A Critical Biography* (Basingstoke: Macmillan, 1983), p. 2.

30. Neil Bartlett, *Who Was That Man? A Present for Mr Oscar Wilde* (London: Serpent's Tail, 1988), p. 76.

31. Ricks, *Introduction to Housman's Collected Poems and Selected Prose*, p. 7.

32. 'The Name and Nature of Poetry' in Ricks, *Introduction to Housman's Collected Poems and Selected Prose*, pp. 369–70.

33. Julia Kristeva, *The Kristeva Reader*, ed. Toril Moi (Oxford: Oxford University Press, 1986), p. 40.

34. Graves quotes Marcel Proust on the subject: 'A homosexual is not a man who loves homosexuals, but merely a man who, seeing a soldier immediately wants to have him for a friend.' (*A. E. Housman, The Scholar-Poet*, p. 108.) This is quite apart from the semi-professional prostitute status which at least one soldier (Charles Parker) in the Wilde trial appeared to hold (see Ellmann, *Oscar Wilde*, p. 447.) See also Steven Marcus, *The Other Victorians, a Study of Pornography and Sexuality in Mid-Nineteenth Century England* (London: Corgi Books, 1969).

35. Cohen, *Talk on the Wilde Side*, p. 203.

36. Quoted in Page, *A. E. Housman, A Critical Biography*, p. 3.

—Ruth Robbins, "'A very curious construction': Masculinity and the Poetry of A.E. Housman and Oscar Wilde." *Cultural Politics at the Fin de Siècle*. Sally Ledger and Scott MacCracken, eds. (Cambridge: Cambridge University Press, 1995). pp. 137–138, 139, 141–142, 144–152.

## CHRISTOPHER RICKS ON HOUSMAN'S "POETRY OF PROTEST"

[Christopher Ricks' essay considers the uniquely "conservative" ethical position taken by Housman's poetry toward the subject of homosexual desire.]

'Oh who is that young sinner with the handcuffs on his wrists?' In 1895, A. E. Housman dealt swingingly with the imprisonment of Oscar Wilde, whose first trial had been in April and who was sent to Reading Gaol in November. His crime: the giving of homosexual offence. The world's judgment (Housman's poem fiercely urged) is as unjust as taking a man 'to prison for the colour of his hair'.

Why, of all capricious gravamina, did Housman seize upon this? Because, while flamboyantly arbitrary, the colour of one's hair had come to represent just such a cruel perversion of injustice. Arbitrary though punishment for the colour of one's hair is, there was nothing arbitrary about Housman's choosing it as his indictment. For it had become a type of the arbitrarily unjust, and so—itself by way of being a tradition—it was the more sharply fitted to the case, a case where there converged with it another good old English tradition, the punitive repudiation that is now dubbed homophobia.

To bring into play, footnotable play, the precedents *in re* the colour of one's hair, is not only to see Housman's instance of preposterous crime as at once impertinent and pertinent, but to take the measure of the poem's *saeva indignatio*.

Laurence Housman, who in 1937 (a year after his brother's death) respectfully chose to publish this unreleased poem,[1] was right to see it as a poem of protest against society's laws, but he was limited in seeing the poem as that only. The poem's protest, as often in Housman, is partly against that part of life which is society's doing and wrongdoing, but is more largely against all else. Society's laws, yes, but nature's too, and, above all, the laws of 'Whatever brute and blackguard made the world'. This, even a chorus of priests might have to acknowledge:

> Oh wearisome condition of humanity!
> Born under one law, to another bound:
> Vainly begot, and yet forbidden vanity,
> Created sick, commanded to be sound:
> What meaneth Nature by these diverse laws?
> (Fulke Greville, Chorus Sacerdotum, from *Mustapha*)

What meaneth Society by these perverse laws? 'The laws of God, the laws of man' (*Last Poems* XII): there the sway and the swaying constitute the even-handed scales of Housman's handy-dandy.

> Oh who is that young sinner with the handcuffs on his wrists?
> And what has he been after that they groan and shake their fists?
> And wherefore is he wearing such a conscience-stricken air?
> Oh they're taking him to prison for the colour of his hair.
>
> 'Tis a shame to human nature, such a head of hair as his;
> In the good old time 'twas hanging for the colour that it is;
> Though hanging isn't bad enough and flaying would be fair
> For the nameless and abominable colour of his hair.
>
> Oh a deal of pains he's taken and a pretty price he's paid
> To hide his poll or dye it of a mentionable shade;
> But they've pulled the beggar's hat off for the world to see and stare,
> And they're haling him to justice for the colour of his hair.

Now 'tis oakum for his fingers and the treadmill for his feet
And the quarry-gang on Portland in the cold and in the heat,
And between his spells of labour in the time he has to spare
He can curse the God that made him for the colour of his hair.

It was not until thirty years after Laurence Housman published the poem that there appeared—likewise after its author's death—his essay on his brother's love and friendship, 'A. E. Housman's "De Amicitia"'.[2] (The Latin has all the decent lack of obscurity of a learned language.) Laurence Housman's words, which manifest a tender probity, are well-known but they remain unexhausted:

> I do not pretend to know how far my brother continued to accept throughout life, in all circumstances, the denial of what was natural to him, but I do know that he considered the inhibition imposed by society on his fellow-victims both cruel and unjust. That fact is made abundantly plain in the poem which, after considerable hesitation, I decided to publish, even though its literary merit was not high—the one beginning

> 'Oh who is that young sinner with the handcuffs on his wrists?'

It refers quite evidently to those who inescapably, through no fault of their own, are homosexual—having no more power of choice in the matter than a man has about the colour of his hair, which, as the poem says, he may hide out of sight, or dye to a 'more mentionable shade,' but cannot get away from. ( ... )

This is admirably executed, down to the duly dry touch—what with prison and infringements of liberty—of 'That poem he had left me at liberty to publish ...' The brotherly paragraphs are truthful, and yet they are not the whole truth. For Laurence Housman's exclusive emphasis, tripled, upon society ('Imposed by society', 'society's treatment of these unhappy victims of fate', 'social injustice'), has the effect of narrowing the poem's perturbation, as though—were society to be so good as to abolish its prohibitive laws—all would be well. Not so.

> How small, of all that human hearts endure,
> That part which laws or kings can cause or cure.[4]

Samuel Johnson, like A. E. Housman, was a radical conservative, and Johnson's great apophthegm, aware of society's injustices, is aware too of life's condition.

For one reason why 'Oh who is that young sinner ...' should not be seen only as social protest is its famously being a sombre pendant to two poems which Housman did publish, next year (1896), consecutively too: *A Shropshire Lad* XLIV, 'Shot? so quick, so clean an ending?', and XLV, 'If it chance your eye offend you'. ( ... )

When Housman congratulates this dead young man, it is with no sense, no implication, that the man had been wrong to feel shame at his sexual self.

> Shot? so quick, so clean an ending?
>   Oh that was right, lad, that was brave:
> Yours was not an ill for mending,
>   'Twas best to take it to the grave.

Housman these days is liable to find himself harshly judged by the new censoriousness that has replaced the old much worse one; his shade may be told that he was a household traitor to his sexual nature (and others') by lacking pride in being 'gay'. Out, out. But Housman wrote what he meant; the poem praises the young man for doing something not only 'brave' but 'right'; and when it goes on immediately 'Yours was not an ill for mending', there is no reason to suppose that for the poet, in this poem or elsewhere, the ill *was* an ill for mending, being after all not truly an ill at all but only deemed so by a social injustice that the mending of man's laws would rectify. It is not social condemnation only that gives such balanced obduracy to Housman's line 'Souls undone, undoing others', or to the stanza that had set the soul before us:

> Oh soon, and better so than later
>   After long disgrace and scorn,
> You shot dead the household traitor,
>   The soul that should not have been born.

There are the clean lines of admiration:

> Undishonoured, clear of danger,
>   Clean of guilt, pass hence and home.

But the admiration is along lines which invoke honour (a magnificently positive double negative, 'Undishonoured'), an invocation that resists any emancipated or enlightened insistence that there is in homosexuality no dishonour or guilt of which one should yearn to be 'clean'. So too, Housman's ensuing poem, *A Shropshire Lad* XLV, comes to an end in praise of the healthy courage that had brought itself to put an end, not to something which was not really sick at all (merely deemed so, socially, wrongly), but to soul-sickness:

> And if your hand or foot offend you,
>> Cut it off, lad, and be whole;
> But play the man, stand up and end you,
>> When your sickness is your soul.

The Biblical injunction to be willing to inflict upon oneself the cutting-off of hand or foot is inestimably more grave than to cut one's hair or 'dye it of a mentionable shade'. But 'the colour of his hair' constitutes a tradition, secular and Biblical, that is germane to the conviction that Housman's poem, tragically, should not be restricted to social protest.

NOTES

1. *A.E.H.* (1937), p. 226: *Additional Poems* XVIII.
2. Annotated by John Carter, *Encounter*, vol. xxix no. 4, October 1967. Laurence Housman had died in 1959.
4. Among the lines supplied by Johnson for Goldsmith's *The Traveller*.

—Christopher Ricks, "A.E. Housman and 'the colour of his hair.'" *Essays in Criticism* 47:3, July 1997: pp. 240–245.

# HELL GATE:
## HOUSMAN'S PERSONAL ALLEGORY

### CRITICAL ANALYSIS OF

# *Last Poems* 31

"Hell Gate," published as poem 31 in *Last Poems*, has been considered one of the more atypical poems in Housman's oeuvre. Not only is it a relatively long piece, but its narrative technique is far less elliptical than many of Housman's other poems. Its simple, direct, rhyming couplets are reminiscent of eighteenth-century narrative poetry, as well as the mythologized setting, which lend *Hell Gate* a quality of eighteenth-century narrative verse. In addition, the poem, to some extent, "paraphrases" the romantic journey or *agon*, recapitulating sources in Dante, Milton, and later nineteenth-century poets such as Blake, Keats, Shelley, Byron, Tennyson, and Browning.

In "Hell Gate," the speaker is led by a "dark conductor" through the underworld, a journey that echoes similar episodes in classical myth and Dante. The poem is thus epic in feeling, for the speaker recounts his life and past experiences—all of what we, as readers, have experienced vicariously through the *Shropshire Lad* poems:

> battle, and the loves of men
> Cities entered, oceans crossed,
> Knowledge gained and virtue lost

He also confronts his prospective future in the form of the sentinel, Ned, who has preceded him down

> the lovely way that led
> To the slimepit and the mire
> And the everlasting fire.

While we are never told why the speaker is sentenced to an afterlife of everlasting fire, earlier poems in *A Shropshire Lad* and *Last Poems* can certainly provide some clues. The tension between desire and social duty—or the strange conflation of both in the image of the soldier—as well as the alienation, emotional distance, and self-reproach that figure in so much of Housman's work culminate here in a life that was not lived properly, whether in the view of society or in that of the speaker. In this respect, "Hell Gate" might be read as a kind of allegory for "Terence Hearsay's" own epic struggle with himself through two volumes of a loosely connected narrative in verse. By extension, we might also read it as a personal allegory for Housman. Unlike previous poems, however, "Hell Gate" is a poem that extends this struggle beyond the realm of thwarted desire or self-destructive fantasy. That is, it addresses the moral and spiritual consequences of these drives, and attempts to move beyond them, within the world of the poem. In this sense, "Hell Gate" is demonstrative of the poet's effort to realize something in poetry that could not be directly confronted, or achieved, in life.

The poem confronts moral tyranny, however, it is interesting that the speaker never questions why he is there. No crime is recounted; merely "the lovely way that led / To the slimepit and the mire." Again, this leaves us to assume that the very nature of this man's life was "the lovely way," rather than any specific event or act he committed. This would be consistent with the tone of this first three stanza as well. When the poet describes the bleakness of Limbo and the intimidating geography of Hell, his voice is emotionally removed from its subject; this may leave the reader with feelings of trepidation and doom, but the speaker remains detached from his surroundings.

However, the poet does engage with Death and Sin on a more personal level. Interestingly, at least one of these figures appears to be female.

> And the portress foul to see
> Lifted up her eyes on me
> Smiling, and I made reply,
> 'Met again, my lass,' said I.

While the speaker may glibly reply to the foul portress's pleasure at his entrance into Hell (and therefore into her power), what better way to disguise fear than with glibness? Moreover, he has encountered "her" before—and this suggests that, for the speaker, either death or sin in the living world involved relationships to women. Take, for example, the soldier fighting for his queen. Or, the lads and lasses of Shropshire—and all of the social conventions they represent—that have caused earlier incarnations of this speaker such frustration, grief, and despair. Earlier in this poem, the burning sentry, in his "finery of fire" is described as "One for women to admire." This is not a trite observation that women like a man in uniform; it suggests, rather, that women can be dangerous. What women desire in a man, and how they and their culture define masculinity, can become some men's undoing, cause them great pain, or even lead them to their deaths.

The sentry, Ned, whom the speaker recognizes as a long-lost friend from the living world, is called to action by their mutual recognition. Ned uses his hell-forged musket and kills the "master"—the "dark porter"—whom we might call the Devil, or tyranny, or the power that spiritual terror exercises over its victims: the fear of sin and death. Thus, what the two friends experienced together in life was a force positive and strong enough to drive Ned to rebellion; perhaps this experience was love. In keeping with this reading, the mutiny is an assertion of freedom and desire, recalling Satan's mutiny in *Paradise Lost*. And just as that Satan felt wrongly condemned by God for his own desires, "Hell Gate" suggests that these men were unjustly damned by some abstract moral or social authority—one which remains unnamed. That this authority is not divine is evidenced by its overthrow, which seems merely to require a will to freedom, for this very basic, human desire has the power to quench that "everlasting fire."

The musket-shot even supercedes the stroke of "clenched lightning," suggesting that even in the underworld, a human act of rebellion can overpower the rule of (what we assume is) nature. In the poem, Hell is hollow and illusory; like one of Prospero's fantastic creations, "it leaves not a wrack behind." Once the tyranny of "the master," Sin, and Death are gone, so is all trace of hell. Ned and the speaker remain together on the open plain. It is an empty space, a metaphorical blank page, and thus, provides the potential for a renewed life.

Two friends—men who have shared experiences of war, and perhaps love—are left alone with each other. That they have "nothing found to say" suggests that there *is* nothing to say or explain: instead, there is mutual understanding. We might read this understanding as a simple, free acknowledgement. Their emotional connection was intense enough to withstand time and death, and powerful enough to destroy moral and spiritual tyranny. Moreover, retracing their steps from the netherworld begins the process of repair, as Ned's clothes of flame fade back into "spruce attire."

Mirroring the opening stanza, the final stanza alludes to classical mythology, Dante, and the Bible. However, just as the setting of the poem is the underworld—a place unlike and *under* the living world, thus "upside-down"—so these allusions are ironic twists, reversing the narrative of their sources. "Midmost of the homeward track" echoes the first lines of Dante's *Inferno*. Rather than a middle-aged man stopping in a forest where two paths diverged, here two middle-aged friends walk along one path towards home. Looking back on Sodom and Gomorrah, Lot's wife was turned to salt; looking back into the underworld, Orpheus lost his wife Eurydice forever. The speaker and his friend look back only to find the city "dusk and mute" while they walk calmly away. This ironic use of poetic allusion signals a change in the poem's setting, a shift in its tone and emotional trajectory, and perhaps a transformation in the speaker.

> But the city, dusk and mute
> Slept, and there was no pursuit.

Muteness, the inability to verbalize or speak, is an interesting choice of words, for it reminds us of the power of language. In "Hell Gate," Housman has made use of this power to convey what, by the poem's conclusion, ironically needs not saying, just as the two friends need not explain themselves to each other. The image of sudden peace and silence surrounding "two friends alone" on a blank plain seems enough to suggest a rather minimal, but healthy, comfort—even, perhaps, a kind of hope. No more self-recrimination or frustrated desire: the speaker in this poem has found some serenity "beneath the nether sky" without the fear of demonic pursuit—either from without, or from within.

## Tom Burns Haber on the Literary Sources for "Hell Gate"

[In this excerpt, Tom Burns Haber considers "Hell Gate" "atypical" style and poetics of the poem, and discusses the work's literary allusions and possible sources.]

There is strong evidence that [Housman] had a specific narrative poem in mind as he composed his longest piece in *Last Poems*, the gloomy fantasia, "Hell Gate." The central theme—comradely love will prevail against the gates of hell itself—is fitting enough; yet as a whole the poem is atypical. Beside its unexampled length (104 lines), there is its peculiar verse-structure used only here and in one other poem: octosyllabic couplets set to trochaic rhythm.

These outward and obvious particulars might declare themselves at once to the most casual reader. But that same reader would probably feel in "Hell Gate" other qualities that make it stand out as an odd number. Housman himself had deep misgivings about the poem. In a letter (already mentioned) asking his former colleague of University College, J. W. Mackail, to criticize the proofsheets of *Last Poems*, Housman remarked the length of the poem might not be "its worst fault", and he added that Mackail should be severely candid in his judgment of it "—not afraid of stifling a masterpiece through a temporary aberration of judgment." Housman concluded by saying that he was putting the suspect poem through the fire of the opinions of "one or two other people."[14]

Part of the unlucky hang of the poem arises, I believe, from the reader's sense that the poem is in some way incomplete, that some important antecedents are missing. This feeling arises in the very first line, where we are told of a road that led onward again. The word *again* sets up an inquiry which holds like an unresolved chord throughout the reading of the poem and recurs as often as we think of the word. Where had the road begun? Where had the travelers set foot on it? How had they met? Reasons for the persistence of these queries, if not their answers, might be found if we knew of a source or sources from which Housman had derived some elements of his story.[15]

A few of these are easily identified: from *Paradise Lost* come the grim warders, Sin and Death; the flaming sentinel and the infernal firearms—not to mention the setting and description of the city of Hell. I also suggest that Robert Browning's "Childe Roland to the Dark Tower Came" might be responsible for the heightening of some descriptive features of the blasted landscape, the lauding of soldierly fidelities, and the survival of the undaunted traveler in a moment of supreme danger.

It was not only its length that made the poem so long in the making; begun about 1905, it was not completed until the summer of 1922—just in time to be included in *Last Poems*. Housman spread three labored drafts (of which only the first and third survive) of this poem over eleven pages of his last notebook, mingling in a way unusual for him both ink and pencil in successive couplets as tentative and final parts of the poem came to him. These various peculiarities, internal and external, combine to raise the question: Is there a model for "Hell Gate"? If one could be found, an explanation of some of the oddities of. the piece might not be far to seek.

There is a definite source for "Hell Gate." It is the poem "Si Descendero in Infernum Ades," written in octosyllabic couplets and trochaic verse by an almost forgotten Victorian poet, George Augustus Simcox, who published it in his *Poems and Romances* (1869). Housman may have known Simcox was also a Classical scholar, but it was by his poetry that he was introduced to the young collegian; for *Poems and Romances* went with Alfred to Oxford, and from it he copied long passages into his commonplace book.

Briefly, the substance of Simcox' 295-line romance is this: Part 1: Lady Rosalie lies dead in a church by the sea. A supernatural element enters:

> And there waited through the night,
> Housed with silk, a steed of might,
> Half of gold and half of fire,
> Shod and bridled with desire.

A knight, the lady's paramour, comes to take her away. Victor rouses her, rebukes her fears, and they ride off together. Part II: On their journey they pass the place of their sinful love-tryst. They are home over the sea; and mention is made of a divine presence that goes with them:

... One with drooping bead,
Following ever as they fled,
Bleeding as He too were slain,
With one hand upon the rein.

They pass "the isle of evil graves" where Victor had lured Rosalie's father to death. His spirit joins them as the steed plunges with the two riders to the deeps of hell undersea. Part III: It is in this part that the important situation is found. The section opens:

So they came unto the city
Of the king who hath no pity;
And that city needs for light
Sun by day nor moon by night;
It is lighted in such wise
By the king's devouring eyes,
Flashing through the dusky air,
For the eyes are everywhere.
And we call the city Hell,
But the people there who dwell
Name it by another name,
And no man may speak the same.
And the golden gates of it,
Where the purple shadows flit,
Where the mighty warders sit,
Are not shut by night or day.

The lovers, their supernatural companions still with them, are welcomed by the angel Azazel. Rosalie asks her father's spirit who the other is and is told it is the Christ. They stand before the throne of the King of Hell, but Rosalie is oblivious of all around her except

Only One who walked the night
Clad upon with tender light,
With a visage pale and sweet,
And with pierced hands and feet,
Saying, "Staunch My wounded side
With more kisses, O My bride!
For the shadows flee away
Into everlasting day."

Thus the poem ends with the veiled conclusion that divine love pardons the errors of human love and saves the faithful even in the very gate of Hell. So, *mutatis mutandis*, in "Hell Gate" Ned, who was also the silent comrade in "The West" (*LP* 1) and is now a taciturn guard of the desolate city, risks all for his friend, kills the Dark Conductor, and saves them both. This act of rescue is such as would become the idealized Moses Jackson, here and elsewhere in Housman's poetry his partner in fictive dangers.

NOTES

14. From a letter dated July 18, 1922, thanking Mackail for agreeing to read the proofs of *Last Poems*. In a second letter dated one week later, Housman returned to his misgiving about "Hell Gate": "the whole thing is on the edge of the absurd."

15. The experiences of a soul being escorted by Hermes to the afterworld Housman had developed in his long poem "The Merry Guide" (*ASL* 42), written perhaps fifteen years before the earliest draft of "Hell Gate."

—Tom Burns Haber, *A.E. Housman*. (New York: Twayne Publishers, 1967). pp. 165–168.

## ROBERT K. MARTIN ON "THE 'REVOLUTIONARY' HOUSMAN"

[Robert K. Martin continues his discussion of Housman's differing strategies in *A Shropshire Lad* and *Last Poems*, focusing here on the poet's "revolutionary" re-imagining of rebellion and redemption in "Hell Gate," and considering the statement that this poem, in the context of *A Shropshire Lad* and *Last Poems*, makes about creativity.]

The most significant manifestation of the "revolutionary" Housman is "Hell Gate," in which he turns again to the model of Milton; but the Milton called upon here is not the pastoral elegist of *Lycidas* but the epic poet of *Paradise Lost*—and that poem is reimagined in a Romantic way. The speaker reaches Hell, only to find that the sentry guarding the gate is an old soldier friend named Ned. Greeting his old friend, the sentry is now transformed into a "flaming mutineer" who kills the master of Hell, and the act of cosmic rebellion leaves the two friends alone, about to begin "the backward way." The expulsion from the Garden becomes the escape from Hell, the revolt against God becomes the revolt against Satan, and the original couple, Adam and Eve, are radically recast as a "pair of friends." The poem is astonishing in its vision of human rebellion against an unjust world. That injustice is no longer some vague notion of Fate, but is, in this collection of poems, specifically seen as the attempt by God and man to impose "foreign laws" to make men "dance as they desire." The poem's role as a trope of homosexual revolt is seen not only in the final emblem of the two friends, but also in the repeated references to the "plain," recalling the Cities of the Plain, and the reference to the moment when the two rebels "looked back," recalling Lot's wife. "There was," however, the poem concludes, "no pursuit." It has been argued the poem is the only one to achieve a "return to the pastoral world" and deals with "the redemption of the fallen world by the innocent world of the past." Although the friends go back, it is back from death to life, not from experience to innocence. There is no suggestion that the pastoral can be restored. The sentry may be an old friend from Shropshire, as it were, but he is a far different figure from the lads of the earlier book. "Hell Gate" is the poem in which Housman imagines that love may conquer death, that man need not accept the fear of damnation, and that evil is vanquished by a transformation of the lad into "the soldier at my side." It is Housman's vision of a triumphant humanity, joined by what Whitman would have called "manly love."

After such a vision, it is hard to imagine that Housman would have returned to the modes of the earlier poems, and indeed he does not. The volume's last poem is called "Fancy's Knell," and it confirms the recognition that death must lead us to life, even more than to art. Unlike the poems of the earlier volume, there is no assurance here that art will survive:

> Away we both must hie,
> To air the ditty,
> And to earth I.

The death of both the individual and the art that he creates leads Housman to a celebration of life, "learn the dances / And praise the tune to-day." Terence refused the call for a dance tune in the penultimate poem of *A Shropshire Lad*; the speaker's concluding image of himself as the flautist in *Last Poems* suggests the distance that has been travelled.

—Robert K. Martin, "A.E. Housman's Two Strategies: *A Shropshire Lad* and *Last Poems*." *The Victorian Newsletter* 66 (1984): p.17.

## B.J. Leggett on the Allegorical Nature of "Hell Gate"

[In this excerpt, B.J. Leggett discusses "Hell Gate's" allegorical significance and its relationship to one of Housman's central themes, pastoral innocence.]

Reading in *Last Poems*, one notes how often the occasion for the poem is the search for the "lost young man," and further how often the poem turns, structurally, on the speaker's sense of his present state in terms of what he remembers of his youth. No poet since Wordsworth, with the possible exception of Thomas, has been so obsessed with the theme of the child as father of the man:

> When first my way to fair I took
>     Few pence in purse had I,
> And long I used to stand and look
>     At things I could not buy.
>
> Now times are altered: if I care
>     To buy a thing I can;
> The pence are here and here's the fair,
>     But where's the lost young man?
>         [*Last Poems* XXXV, ll. 1–8]

The poems of this type all contain, at bottom, the paradoxical notion that it was only the illusion that made life meaningful. The mature man, in looking into the past, sees that life held a hope and a significance for the young man which he no longer finds. The very act of looking into the past destroys the meaning by revealing the illusion. In "When first my way to fair I took," this idea is suggested in a rather complex way by the contrast between the young man with the few pence for whom the fair held meaning, and the mature man, who could now satisfy the desires of his youth, except that the act would now be meaningless. It was only the vanity and innocence which created the desires (and the meaning), and the young man is gone. The fair itself, vanity fair, implies a view of the world as a kind of empty, glittering facade which attracts the country boy but dissolves into a tawdry sideshow when he returns to it as an adult. The poem's intent is not, however, to reveal the vanity of youthful desires but to suggest the destructive effect of knowledge:

> —To think that two and two are four
>   And neither five nor three
> The heart of man has long been sore
>   And long 'tis like to be.
>
> [ll. 9–12]

Whatever significance the fair held has departed with the lost young man, and the persona's search for meaning takes him back to the past to a meaning which is destroyed by the very act of observing it. The tension between past and present is obviously real for Housman, and it contains the sort of paradox which attracted him.

"Hell Gate" (*Last Poems* XXXI), a poem unlike any other Housman ever wrote, serves almost as an allegory for one aspect of his treatment of the past. In contrast to the poet's customary lyrical mode, "Hell Gate" employs narrative and symbolic devices to treat the convergence of idyllic past and hellish present. As the narrator journeys on the road to hell in the company of his "dark conductor," he reflects on the path which led him there:

> Many things I thought of then,
> Battle, and the loves of men,
> Cities entered, oceans crossed,
> Knowledge gained and virtue lost,
> Cureless folly done and said,
> And the lovely way that led
> To the slimepit and the mire
> And the everlasting fire.
>
> [ll. 25–32]

The sentry, one of the damned who guards the gates of hell, also reminds him of another time and place, and in the company of Death and Sin, "the sentry turned his head, / Looked, and knew me, and was Ned" (ll. 63–64). At the center of the poem is the consequence of this vision from the past for the two old friends. United in hell, they revolt, and Ned turns his musket on the master of hell:

> And the hollowness of hell
> Sounded as its master fell,
> And the mourning echo rolled
> Ruin through his kingdom old.
> Tyranny and terror flown

Left a pair of friends alone,
And beneath the nether sky
All that stirred was he and I.
[ll. 87–94]

Then, silently, "nothing found to say," the two friends from the past begin "the backward way," and the hell-fire which has covered Ned begins to fade:

And the ebbing lustre died
From the soldier at my side,
As in all his spruce attire
Failed the everlasting fire.
Midmost of the homeward track
Once we listened and looked back;
But the city, dusk and mute,
Slept, and there was no pursuit.
[ll. 97–104]

Clearly the poem deals with a recurring theme of *A Shropshire Lad* and *Last Poems*, a longing for the redemption of the fallen world by the innocent world of the past. It is a theme which could not be treated realistically, but the surrealistic atmosphere of "Hell Gate" allows the poet to realize a vision which is always destroyed in the surrounding lyrics of *Last Poems*—the return to the pastoral world of the early Shropshire poems. Ned, the symbol of that world, releases the persona from the hold of Death and Sin, the hell to which the fall from innocence has led him. At the end of the poem the two friends are on a "homeward track." The narrator has recovered the "lost young man," but only in a dream-vision.

—B.J. Leggett, *The Poetic Art of A.E. Housman: Theory and Practice.* (Lincoln, Nebraska: University of Nebraska Press, 1978): pp.79–81.

WORKS BY
# A.E. Housman

## POETRY

*A Shropshire Lad*, 1896.
*Last Poems*, 1922.
*More Poems*, 1936.
*The Manuscript Poems of A.E. Housman*, ed. Tom Burns Haber, 1955.
*The Collected Poems of A.E. Housman*, ed. J. Carter, 1939.
*The Making of A Shropshire Lad: A Manuscript Variorum*, ed. Tom Burns Haber, 1966.
*The Works of A.E. Housman: With an Iintroduction and Bibliography*, 1994.
*The Poems of A.E. Housman*, ed. Archie Burnett, 1997.
*Collected Poems and Selected Prose*, ed. Christopher Ricks, 1989.


## PROSE

*Nine Essays*, by Arthur Platt, with a preface by A. E. Housman, 1927.
*Fragment of a Greek Tragedy*, 1883.
*Introductory Lecture*, 1937 (privately printed 1892).
*The Name and the Nature of Poetry*, 1933.
*The Confines of Criticism: The Cambridge Inaugural*, 1911.
*The Confines of Criticism*, 1969.
*Selected Prose*, ed. John Carter, 1961.
*The Classical Papers of A.E. Housman*, 3 Vols, eds J. Carter, J. Diggle, and F.R.D. Goodyear, 1972.


## LETTERS

*A.E. Housman to Joseph Ishill: five unpublished letters*, ed. William White, 1959.
*Thirty Housman letters to Witter Bynner*, ed. Tom Burns Haber, 1957.
*The Letters of A.E. Housman*, 1971.

# WORKS ABOUT
# A.E. Housman

Auden, W.H. *Victorian and Edwardian Poets: Tennyson to Yeats.* Pearson, Norman Holmes, ed. New York: Viking, 1957.

Birch, J. Roy and Alan W. Holden. *A.E. Housman: A Reassessment.* New York: Macmillan, 2000.

Birch, J. Roy and Archie Burnett. *Unkind to Unicorns: Comic Verse of A.E. Housman.* Bromsgrove: Housman Society, 1999.

Bourne, Jeremy. *"Soldier, I wish you well": the Military Poems of A.E. Housman and the Letters from Burma of G.H. Housman.* Bromsgrove : Housman Society, 2001.

———. *The Westerly Wanderer: A Brief Portrait of A.E. Housman Author of 'A Shropshire lad' 1896–1996.* Bromsgrove: Housman Society, 1996.

Bruce, Sylvia. Essays on Isak Dinesen and A.E. Housman. West Bridgford: Paupers' Press, 1994.

Carter, John and John Hanbury Angus Sparrow. *A.E. Housman; an Annotated Hand-List.* London: R. Hart-Davis, 1952.

———. and William White. *A.E. Housman, a Bibliography.* Godalming, Surrey: St. Paul's Bibliographies, 1982.

Carter, John; Scott, Joseph William. *A.E. Housman; Catalogue of an Exhibition on the Centenary of his Birth.* London: University College, London, 1959.

Chambers, R. W. *Man's Unconquerable Mind; Studies of English Writers, from Bede to A.E. Housman and W.P. Ker.* London: Cape, 1955.

Clucas, Humphrey. *Through Time and Place to Roam: Essays on A.E. Housman.* Salzburg, University of Salzburg, 1995.

Efrati, Carol. *The Road of Danger, Guilt, and Shame: The Lonely Way of A.E. Housman.* Cranbury, NJ: Fairleigh Dickinson University Press, 2002.

Gardner, Philip, ed. *A.E. Housman, the Critical Heritage.* New York : Routledge, 1992.

Gow, Andrew Sydenham Farrar. *A.E. Housman; a Sketch Together with a List of His Writings and Indexes to His Classical Papers.* Folcroft, PA.: Folcroft Library Editions, 1973, 1936.

Graves, Richard Perceval. *A.E. Housman: The Scholar-Poet.* Oxford: Oxford University Press, 1981.

Hawkins, Maude. *A.E. Housman: Man Behind a Mask*. Chicago: Henry Regnery Company, 1958.

Hoagwood, Terence Allan. *A.E. Housman Revisited*. New York: Twayne Publishers, 1995.

Housman, Laurence. "A Poet in the Making." *Atlantic*. Vol. 178, no. 1 (July, 1946).

———. *My Brother, A.E. Housman*. Port Washington, N.Y.: Kennikat Press, 1969.

———. *My Brother, A.E. Housman: Personal Recollections Together with Thirty Hitherto Unpublished Poems*. New York: Charles Scribner's Sons, 1938.

Jebb, Keith. *A.E. Housman*. Bridgend, Mid Glamorgan: Seren Books, 1992.

Ledger, Sally and Scott McCracken. *Cultural Politics at the* Fin de Siècle. Cambridge: Cambridge University Press, 1995.

Leggett, B. J. *Housman's Land of Lost Content; a Critical Study of* A Shropshire Lad. Knoxville: University of Tennessee Press, 1970.

———. *The Poetic Art of A.E. Housman: Theory and Practice*. Lincoln: University of Nebraska Press, 1978.

Marlow, Norman. *A.E. Housman*. Minneapolis: University of Minnesota Press, 1958.

Millard, Kenneth. *Edwardian Poetry*. Oxford: Oxford University Press, 1991.

Naiditch, P.G. *A.E. Housman at University College, London: the Election of 1892*. New York: E.J. Brill, 1988.

Page, Norman. *A.E. Housman: A Critical Biography*. London: Macmillan, 1996.

Platnauer, Maurice. *Variants in the Manuscripts of the Poems of Rupert Brook and A.E. Housman*. London: Oxford University Press, 1943.

Quinn, Kenneth. *Method in Criticism from A.E. Housman to Susan Sontag*. Sydney: University of Sydney, 1982.

Ricks, Christopher B. *A.E. Housman*. Englewood Cliffs, N.J.: Prentice-Hall 1968.

———. *The Force of Poetry*. New York : Clarendon Press, 1984.

Robinson, Oliver. *Angry Dust, the Poetry of A.E. Housman; a Critical Essay*. Boston: Humphries, 1950.

Scott-Kilvert, Ian. *A.E. Housman*. London: Longmans, Green, 1965.

———. *British Writers.Volume 6, Thomas Hardy to Wilfred Owen*. New York: Charles Scribner's Sons, 1983.

Squire, John Collings, Sir. *Essays on Poetry*. New York: George H. Doran, 1924.

Stallman, R. W. *Annotated Bibliography of A.E. Housman: a Critical Study*. New York: Modern Language Association of America, 1945.

Stanford, Donald E. *British Poets, 1880–1914*. Detroit: Gale Research Co., 1983.

Tinker, Chauncey Brewster. *Essays in Retrospect: Collected Articles and Addresses*. New Haven: Yale University Press, 1966.

Watson, George L. *A.E. Housman; a Divided Life*. Folcroft, Pa.: Folcroft Library Editions, 1972.

White, William M. *A.E. Housman: An Annotated Check-list; Additions and Corrections; III* London: The Bibliographical Society, 1952.

Young, Robyn V. *Poetry Criticism: Volume 2, Excerpts from Criticism of the Works of the Most Significant and Widely Studied Poets of World Literature*. Detroit: Gale Research Inc., 1991.

# ACKNOWLEDGMENTS

"The Divided Self in the Poems of A.E. Housman" by Ellen Friedman. From *English Literature in Transition*, 1880–1920 20:1, 1997. © 1977 by Ellen Friedman. Reprinted by permission of the author.

"Housman's Loveliest of Trees" by Miriam B. Mandel. From the *Housman Society Journal*, 14, 1988. © 1988 by Miriam B. Mandel. Reprinted by permission.

"A.E. Housman's 'Level Tones'" by Archie Burnett. From *A.E. Housman: A Reassessment*, Alan W. Holden and J. Roy Birch, eds. (New York: St. Martin's Press, 2000). © 2000 by Alan W. Holden and J. Roy Birch. Reprinted by permission of Palgrave Macmillan.

*A.E. Housman* by Keith Jebb (The Cromwell Press Limited, 1992). © 1992 by Keith Jebb. Reprinted by permission.

"The Poetry of A.E. Housman" by Holbrook Jackson. From *A.E. Housman: The Critical Heritage* (Routledge, 1992). Originally printed in *Today* V, August 1919. © 1919 by Holbrook Jackson. Reprinted by permission.

"Alfred Edward Housman" by Cleanth Brooks. From *A.E. Housman: A Collection of Critical Essays* (Englewood Cliffs, NJ: Prentice Hall, 1968). © 1968 by Prentice Hall. Reprinted by permission.

"Horatian Tradition and Pastoral Mode in Housman's A Shropshire Lad" by R.L. Kowalczyk. From *Victorian Poetry* IV: 4, 1966. © 1966 by R.L. Kowalczyk. Reprinted by permission.

*The Poetic Art of A. E. Housman: Theory and Practice* by B.J. Leggett (University of Nebraska Press, 1978). © 1978 by University of Nebraska Press. Reprinted by permission.

"Alfred Edward Housman" by Cleanth Brooks. From *A.E. Housman: A Collection of Critical Essays* (Englewood Cliffs, NJ: Prentice Hall, 1968). © 1968 by Prentice Hall. Reprinted by permission.

"The Nature of Housman's Poetry" by Christopher Ricks. From *A.E. Housman: A Collection of Critical Essays* (Englewood Cliffs, NJ: Prentice Hall, 1968). © 1968 by Prentice Hall. Reprinted by permission.

# INDEX OF
# Themes and Ideas